Access My eLab leap 2

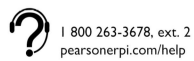

TO REGIS[TER]

1. Go to **mybookshelf.pearsonerpi.com**
2. Follow the instructions. When asked for your access code, please type the code provided underneath the blue sticker.
3. To access **My eLab** at any time, go to http://mybookshelf.pearsonerpi.com. **Bookmark this page for quicker access.**

Access to My eLab is valid for 12 months from the date of registration.

[redacted]

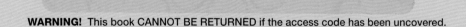

WARNING! This book CANNOT BE RETURNED if the access code has been uncovered.

Note: Once you have registered, you will need to join your online class. Ask your teacher to provide you with the class ID.

TEACHER Access Code

To obtain an access code for My eLab, please contact your Pearson ELT consultant.

1 800 263-3678, ext. 2
pearsonerpi.com/help

W139667 (A39668)

3265

leap 2

NEW EDITION

LISTENING AND SPEAKING

DR. KEN BEATTY

Pearson

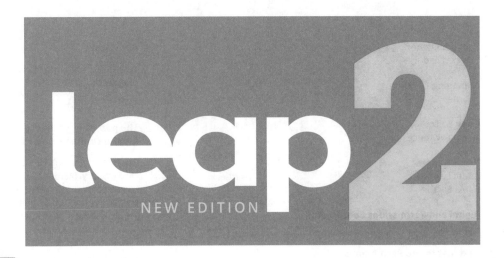

Product Owner
Stephan Leduc

Managing Editor
Sharnee Chait

Copy Editor
Adam Lawrence

Proofreaders
Adam Lawrence
Paula Sarson

Rights and Permissions Coordinator
Aude Maggiori

Text Rights and Permissions
Rachel Irwin

Art Director
Hélène Cousineau

Graphic Design Manager
Estelle Cuillerier

Book and Cover Design
Frédérique Bouvier

Book Layout
Isabel Lafleur

Cover Photos
Shutterstock © InnervisionArt
Shutterstock © Rawpixel.com

ERPI publishes and distributes PEARSON ELT products in Canada.

1611 Crémazie Boulevard East, 10th Floor
Montréal, Québec H2M 2P2
Canada
Telephone: 1 800 263-3678
Fax: 514 334-4720
information@pearsonerpi.com
pearsonerpi.com

Registration of copyright – Bibliothèque et Archives nationales du Québec, 2019
Registration of copyright – Library and Archives Canada, 2019

Printed in Canada

ISBN 978-2-7613-9667-7 123456789 HLN 22 21 20 19
(82021429) 139667 ABCD OF10

Dedication

To all those with the courage to learn a new language; it's a long but pleasing path.

The publisher wishes to thank the following people for their helpful comments and suggestions:

Carrie Barr, Queen's University
Nicole Bailey, Memorial University
Louise Lemieux, University of British Columbia
Natalie Penney-Toba, Memorial University
Joy L. Salzberg, University of British Columbia

Special thanks are due to the following instructors from Fraser International College for their extensive feedback:

Jerry Block, Sheena Bhatia, Stephanie Marie Breck, Rosa Maria Funderburk Razo, Winnie Ma, Yvonne Muir, David Puddiford, Jane Rogers, Liz Rogers, Linda Yauk, and Dani Zheleva

INTRODUCTION

Welcome to the new edition of *LEAP 2: Listening and Speaking*. Building on the first edition (*LEAP Intermediate*), this book aims to improve your listening and speaking skills with Academic Word List (AWL) vocabulary, grammar, Academic Survival Skills, and Warm-Up and Final Assignments that let you apply what you learn in individual and personalized ways.

There are two new features in *LEAP 2: Listening and Speaking*. Focus on Critical Thinking helps you reflect on what you listen to so you can develop your own opinions. The Pearson Global Scale of English (GSE) structures *LEAP 2*'s learning goals to give you a clearer idea of the language objectives you should aim to meet.

Each chapter in the book focuses on engaging themes drawn from science, technology, engineering, and mathematics (STEM), as well as the education and business fields. Each chapter includes three listenings related to the chapter theme, often with divergent perspectives. Most of these listenings are authentic and give you the chance to apply your critical thinking skills in pre-listening and follow-up tasks. The listenings, including at least one video per chapter, cover a variety of genres that you will encounter in your academic studies, including lectures, interviews, and podcasts. The speaking component involves different types of presentations and participation in seminars and debates. Beyond the book, My eLab exercises and documents give you the opportunity to reinforce and build on what you learn.

LEAP 2: Listening and Speaking will give you the confidence to take the next steps on your path to academic and career success.

ACKNOWLEDGEMENTS

As always, my thanks to Julia Williams who started this series. With patience and good humour, my editor Sharnee Chait has made the writing process more enjoyable; I thank her and the rest of the Pearson team who brought my words to life and put them in the hands of teachers. I also thank my graduate students and colleagues for ongoing discussions that reinforce my belief that student needs are the starting point for everything important in education.

The influence of teachers too numerous to name are found on these pages. Creating *LEAP 2: Listening and Speaking* began with exploring teacher and student needs and finding creative solutions to meet the changing demands of academic English. Consultations with teachers internationally helped fuel the ideas for this book. I appreciate the thoughtful contributions of those dedicated professionals who offered feedback through questionnaires and chapter reviews. I particularly thank those teachers who emailed me and whom I met at conferences, lectures, and workshops this past year in Argentina, Canada, Chile, Colombia, Czech Republic, England, Poland, Slovakia, Uruguay, and the US. Every teacher is a hero.

Dr. Ken Beatty, Bowen Island, Canada

HIGHLIGHTS

Gearing Up uses infographics to spark critical thinking, reflection, and discussion about the chapter topic.

The **overview** outlines the chapter's objectives and features.

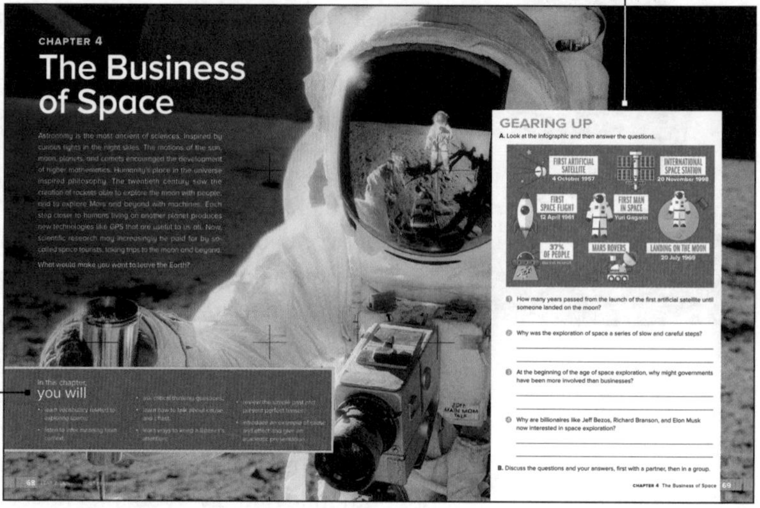

Vocabulary Build strengthens comprehension and builds awareness of key vocabulary on the Academic Word List.

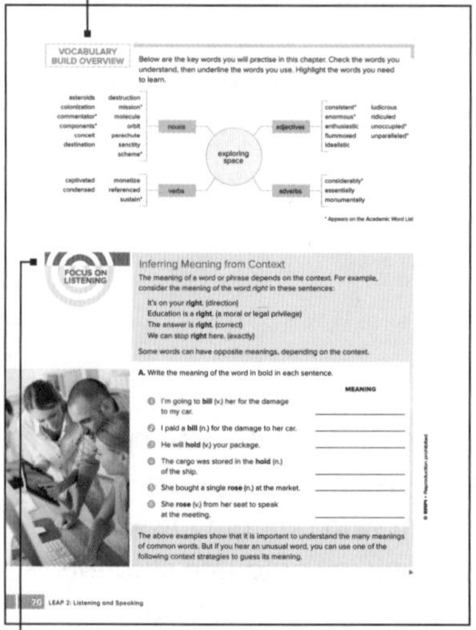

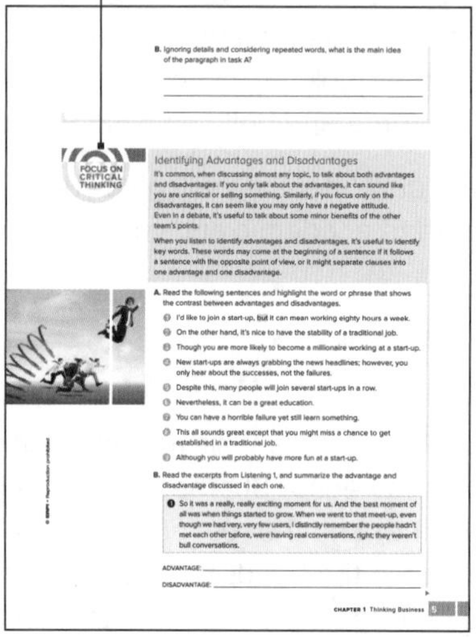

Focus on Critical Thinking helps you learn strategies for thinking critically about what you hear and ways to apply these strategies to listening and speaking tasks.

Before, **while**, and **after listening** activities elicit prior knowledge, engage you in active listening strategies, and focus on comprehension and critical thinking.

Focus on Listening develops specific strategies you need to fully understand the content and structure of different listening genres.

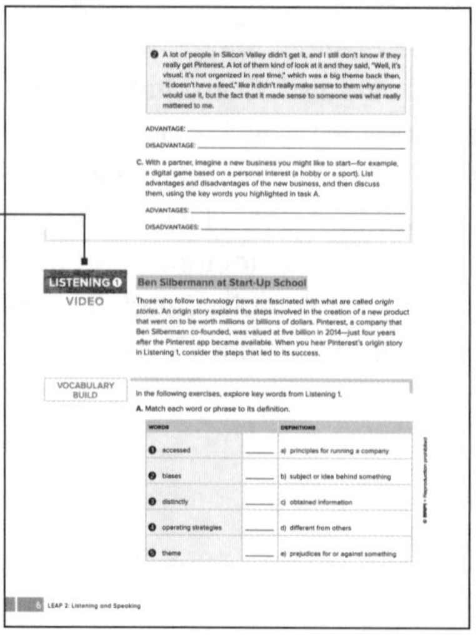

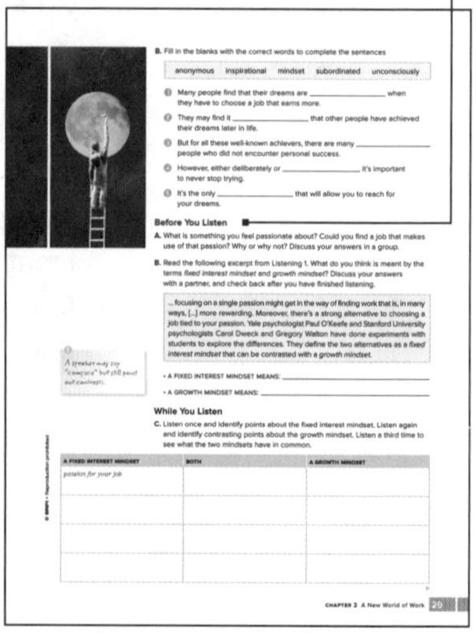

Each chapter contains three **listenings**, including at least one video, which come from a variety of sources: lectures, debates, interviews, and podcasts. The listenings offer different perspectives on the chapter theme, providing content for speaking tasks.

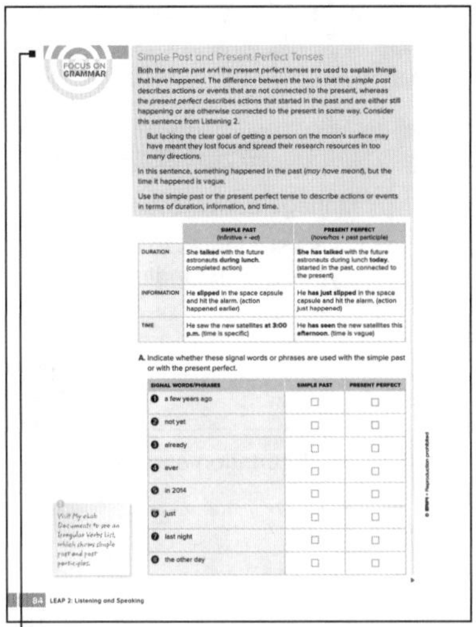

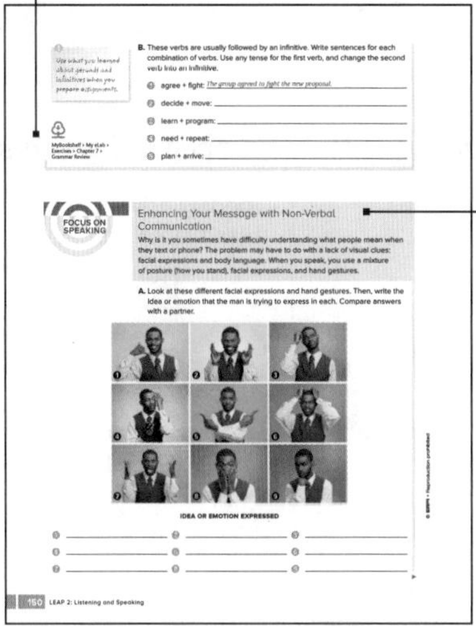

My eLab provides practice and additional content.

Focus on Speaking develops specific skills you need to effectively discuss issues using academic English.

Focus on Grammar reviews important structures that you can apply when listening and speaking academic English.

Academic Survival Skill helps you develop essential skills for academic coursework.

The **Warm-Up Assignment** prepares you for the Final Assignment. Each chapter focuses on a different task.

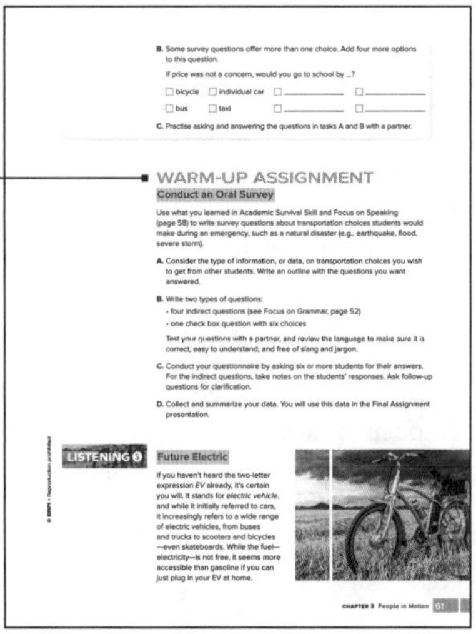

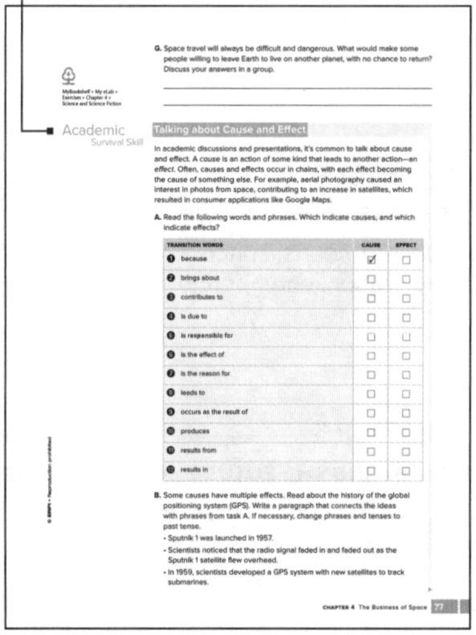

The **Final Assignment** synthesizes the chapter content and theme into an in-depth speaking task. Each chapter focuses on a different type of assignment.

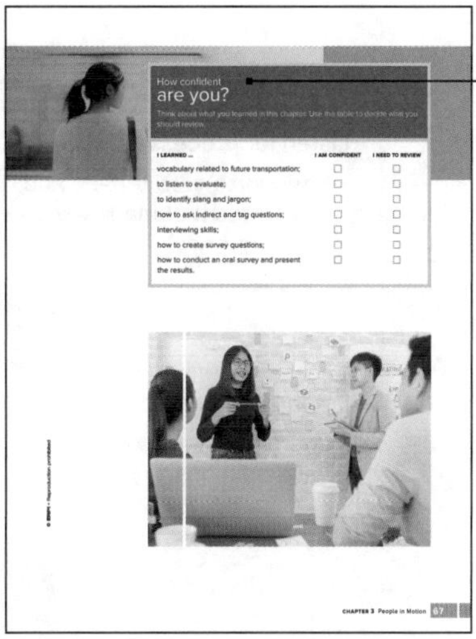

How confident are you? allows you to reflect on your learning and decide what you want to review.

SCOPE AND SEQUENCE

CHAPTER	LISTENING	CRITICAL THINKING	SPEAKING
CHAPTER 1 **THINKING BUSINESS** SUBJECT AREAS: business, computing, technology	• Listen for the main idea - Learn strategies	• Identify advantages and disadvantages - Listen for key words	• Manage conversations - Use strategies to improve your understanding
CHAPTER 2 **A NEW WORLD OF WORK** SUBJECT AREAS: business, education, technology	• Listen for compare and contrast - Identify phrases	• Use active listening strategies	• Use intonation and stress
CHAPTER 3 **PEOPLE IN MOTION** SUBJECT AREAS: engineering, urban planning	• Listen to evaluate - Learn listening strategies	• Identify slang and jargon - Use strategies to decide when to use slang or jargon	• Learn interviewing skills - Review closed- and open-ended questions
CHAPTER 4 **THE BUSINESS OF SPACE** SUBJECT AREAS: space exploration, engineering	• Listen to infer meaning from context - Learn context strategies	• Ask critical thinking questions - Analyze a speaker's ideas and messages	• Keep a listener's attention - Use emotional words and vary sentences
CHAPTER 5 **INVENTING THE FUTURE** SUBJECT AREAS: computing, engineering	• Listen for point of view - Learn ways to predict and interpret a speaker's point of view	• Build schema - Improve your understanding while you listen	• Use register and tone - Learn about different registers and choosing your words
CHAPTER 6 **ENGINEERING THE FUTURE** SUBJECT AREAS: engineering, medicine	• Predict and infer ideas - Recognize signal words and phrases	• Use thought experiments to explore ideas - Examine positive and negative consequences	• Use aids when speaking - Use visual aids and props
CHAPTER 7 **NEW WAYS TO LEARN** SUBJECT AREAS: computer science, education	• Listen for processes - Recognize verb tenses and key words that mark stages in a sequence	• Organize ideas into a sequence - Learn about process order and chronological order	• Enhance your message with non-verbal communication - Use facial expressions and body language
CHAPTER 8 **FINDING JUSTICE** SUBJECT AREAS: history, law, technology	• Distinguish fact from opinion - Learn how to recognize valid opinions	• Ask follow-up questions - Use reduced-form questions and paraphrases	• Construct an argument - Learn how to structure your argument

FOR COURSEBOOK AND MY ELAB

VOCABULARY	GRAMMAR	ACADEMIC SURVIVAL SKILL	ASSIGNMENTS
• Explore meaning and context • Find synonyms and word forms	• Review yes/no questions	• Take notes - Learn different ways to take notes	• Work in a group to create an idea for an app • Give a presentation and take notes
• Explore meaning and context • Use suffixes	• Review comparative and superlative form	• Learn how to give a compare and contrast presentation - Review how to cite oral sources	• Describe your perfect job • Give a compare and contrast presentation
• Explore meaning and context • Use prefixes	• Review indirect and tag questions	• Create survey questions - Use closed- and open-ended questions	• Conduct an oral survey • Prepare and present an oral survey
• Explore meaning and context	• Review the simple past and present perfect tenses	• Talk about cause and effect - Identify phrases to indicate causes and effects	• Introduce an example of cause and effect • Give an academic presentation
• Explore meaning and context • Find word forms	• Review sentence types - Identify simple, compound, complex, and compound-complex sentences	• Develop teamwork skills - Learn techniques to work successfully in a team	• Develop product proposals • Conduct a meeting to discuss proposals
• Explore meaning and context • Find word forms	• Review conditional sentences	• Learn to paraphrase and summarize	• Summarize an interview • Participate in a group discussion
• Explore meaning and context • Find root words and word forms	• Review gerunds and infinitives	• Start a discussion with a thesis statement - Learn how to construct a thesis statement	• Give a process presentation • Explain a process in a seminar
• Explore meaning and context	• Review modals that express possibility	• Use debate strategies - Identify logical fallacies	• Construct an argument for a debate • Participate in a debate

TABLE OF CONTENTS

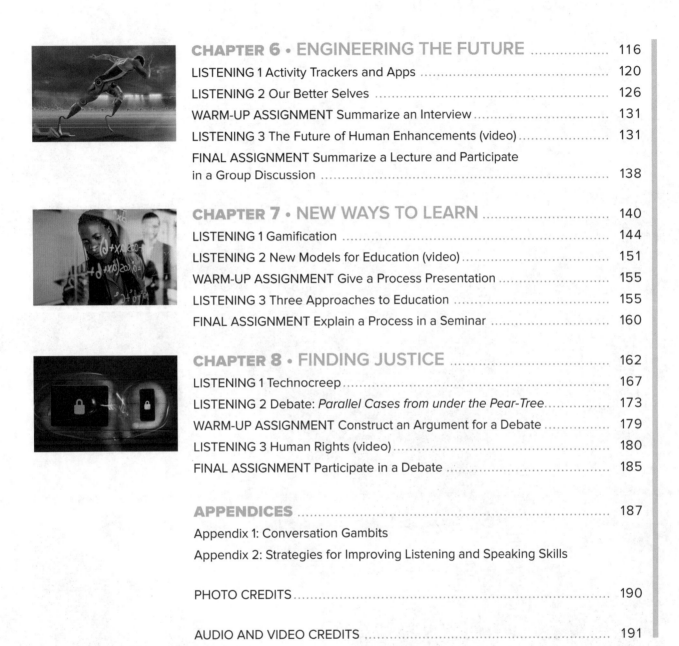

CHAPTER 1

Thinking Business

A hundred years ago, starting a large business involved much more than a good idea. You would build a factory and hire hundreds of employees. The employees would work together to make products and then ship them to shops by truck, train, or boat. But many of today's wealthiest innovators have created businesses that do not require factories, physical products, shipping, or shops. For example, the founders of the online photo-sharing site Instagram created a business with just thirteen employees, then sold it in 2012 for one billion dollars.

Is it any wonder people are interested in different business models?

In this chapter, you will

- learn vocabulary related to new business models;
- listen for the main idea;
- identify advantages and disadvantages;
- organize ideas using note-taking strategies;
- manage conversations;
- review yes/no questions;
- work in a group to create an idea for an app;
- give a presentation and take notes.

GEARING UP

A. Look at the diagram and then answer the questions.

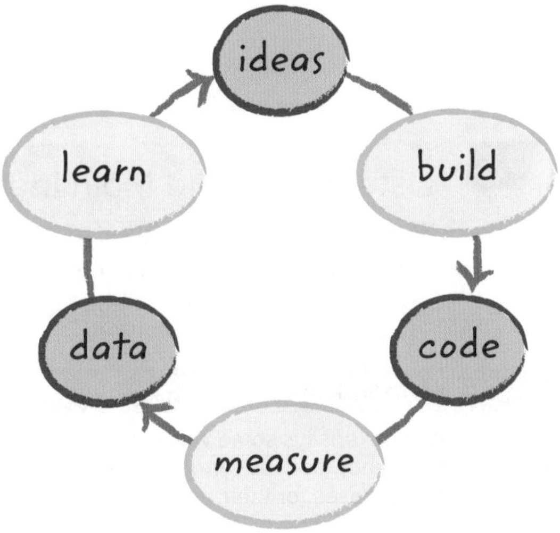

1. A start-up is a new business, often one with a technology focus. A "lean" start-up develops an online business quickly. It is expected that failures will lead to new ideas. Starting with the *ideas* bubble, what do you think each of the stages in the diagram means?

   ____

   ____

   ____

   ____

2. Which stages do you think are the easiest, and which are the most difficult? Why?

   ____

   ____

3. Instagram's success was based on a friend's suggestion to include filters that could modify and re-colour photos. Where in the diagram would you place that suggestion?

   ____

   ____

B. Discuss the questions and your answers, first with a partner, then in a group.

VOCABULARY BUILD OVERVIEW

Below are the key words you will practise in this chapter. Check the words you understand, then underline the words you use. Highlight the words you need to learn.

new business models

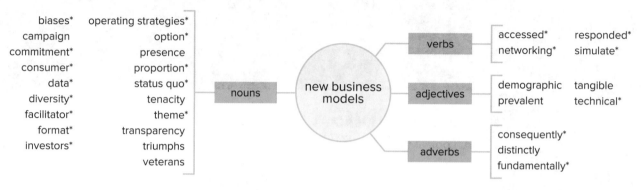

nouns

biases*, campaign, commitment*, consumer*, data*, diversity*, facilitator*, format*, investors*, operating strategies*, option*, presence, proportion*, status quo*, tenacity, theme*, transparency, triumphs, veterans

verbs

accessed*, networking*, responded*, simulate*

adjectives

demographic, prevalent, tangible, technical*

adverbs

consequently*, distinctly, fundamentally*

* Appears on the Academic Word List

FOCUS ON LISTENING

Listening for the Main Idea

While you listen to a lecture, try to identify the main idea. Sometimes the main idea is obvious; often, it is introduced in the title. Here are strategies you can use to help you identify a main idea while you listen.

STRATEGIES	EXPLANATIONS	EXAMPLES FROM LISTENING 1
Listen for words and ideas that are repeated.	A speaker says some words more frequently, or uses synonyms and paraphrases for them.	... we weren't great at one **thing**. Right, there wasn't one **thing** that was special ...
Listen for clues from the speaker that tell you some parts of a talk are more important.	A speaker asks questions that will be answered in the talk. A speaker uses words and phrases to indicate that one or more ideas are important.	And **the best** moment of all was, when things started to grow. **The important point is** ... **What I'm trying to say** ...
Listen for changes in pitch and volume.	Words spoken at a higher pitch or in a louder voice signal important ideas.	And we waited until we felt we had something that we thought was really **cool**. So, we're just going to **market** this thing. (Note: Words in bold are said louder or at a higher pitch.)

These key phrases often signal main ideas.

INTRODUCTION: Today, we'll discuss ...
EXCEPTION: However, ...
CAUSE AND EFFECT: Because of this, ...
PARAPHRASE: In other words, ...
EXAMPLE: For example, ...
SUMMARY: In conclusion, ...

A. Finding the main idea involves ignoring unnecessary details. Read this excerpt from Listening 1. Cross out words, phrases, and details you consider unnecessary. Highlight important words that are repeated.

> Somebody asked me once, like what's my big plan? What would make me really happy? When we were starting Pinterest I was like, "Geez, I just want to go somewhere and see somebody that I don't know using something that I made and have it be kind of useful." Like that is what I thought was really exciting. And so, we came up with this idea for something that was Web-based, really simple, something that we would use personally, and that was Pinterest.

B. Ignoring details and considering repeated words, what is the main idea of the paragraph in task A?

____

____

____

FOCUS ON CRITICAL THINKING

Identifying Advantages and Disadvantages

It's common, when discussing almost any topic, to talk about both advantages and disadvantages. If you only talk about the advantages, it can sound like you are uncritical or selling something. Similarly, if you focus only on the disadvantages, it can seem like you may only have a negative attitude. Even in a debate, it's useful to talk about some minor benefits of the other team's points.

When you listen to identify advantages and disadvantages, it's useful to identify key words. These words may come at the beginning of a sentence if it follows a sentence with the opposite point of view, or it might separate clauses into one advantage and one disadvantage.

A. Read the following sentences and highlight the word or phrase that shows the contrast between advantages and disadvantages.

1. I'd like to join a start-up, but it can mean working eighty hours a week.
2. On the other hand, it's nice to have the stability of a traditional job.
3. Though you are more likely to become a millionaire working at a start-up.
4. New start-ups are always grabbing the news headlines; however, you only hear about the successes, not the failures.
5. Despite this, many people will join several start-ups in a row.
6. Nevertheless, it can be a great education.
7. You can have a horrible failure yet still learn something.
8. This all sounds great except that you might miss a chance to get established in a traditional job.
9. Although you will probably have more fun at a start-up.

B. Read the excerpts from Listening 1, and summarize the advantage and disadvantage discussed in each one.

1. So it was a really, really exciting moment for us. And the best moment of all was when things started to grow. When we went to that meet-up, even though we had very, very few users, I distinctly remember the people hadn't met each other before, were having real conversations, right; they weren't bull conversations.

ADVANTAGE: _______________

DISADVANTAGE: _______________

❷ A lot of people in Silicon Valley didn't get it, and I still don't know if they really get Pinterest. A lot of them kind of look at it and they said, "Well, it's visual; it's not organized in real time," which was a big theme back then, "it doesn't have a feed," like it didn't really make sense to them why anyone would use it, but the fact that it made sense to someone was what really mattered to me.

ADVANTAGE: ____________________

DISADVANTAGE: ____________________

C. With a partner, imagine a new business you might like to start—for example, a digital game based on a personal interest (a hobby or a sport). List advantages and disadvantages of the new business, and then discuss them, using the key words you highlighted in task A.

ADVANTAGES: ____________________

DISADVANTAGES: ____________________

LISTENING 1 VIDEO

Ben Silbermann at Start-Up School

Those who follow technology news are fascinated with what are called *origin stories*. An origin story explains the steps involved in the creation of a new product that went on to be worth millions or billions of dollars. Pinterest, a company that Ben Silbermann co-founded, was valued at five billion in 2014—just four years after the Pinterest app became available. When you hear Pinterest's origin story in Listening 1, consider the steps that led to its success.

VOCABULARY BUILD

In the following exercises, explore key words from Listening 1.

A. Match each word or phrase to its definition.

WORDS		DEFINITIONS
❶ accessed	_____	a) principles for running a company
❷ biases	_____	b) subject or idea behind something
❸ distinctly	_____	c) obtained information
❹ operating strategies	_____	d) different from others
❺ theme	_____	e) prejudices for or against something

B. Fill in the blanks with the correct words to complete the paragraph. Use a dictionary to look up words you don't understand.

campaign	data	fundamentally	investors	responded

Throughout history, ____________________ have always ____________________ to market needs by supporting or developing new companies. They are ____________________ interested in creating profits for themselves and others. One way investors have been able to create profits is to take advantage of vast amounts of ____________________. But it's increasingly common for members of the public to start a ____________________ against the use of private data.

Before You Listen

A. Based on the excerpt you read in Focus on Listening (page 4), and on the title and introduction to Listening 1, which questions about Ben Silbermann would you expect to have answered? Write the questions and discuss them with a partner. Then, while you listen, take notes and use them to write complete answers.

1. Who *is Ben Silbermann?*

   Ben Silbermann is a young entrepreneur who co-founded Pinterest.

2. What ____________________

3. When ____________________

4. Where ____________________

5. Why ____________________

6. How ____________________

B. What do you already know about technology start-ups? Discuss in a group.

____

____

____

C. Define the words and phrases in bold based on their context in the paragraph. Look at the surrounding words, definitions, and examples. These words will help you understand Listening 1.

> Many young entrepreneurs are attracted to California's **Silicon Valley** to work in the technology industry. Getting a job can be as easy as connecting with employers attending one or more **meet-ups**. At meet-ups, they can get together with technical-minded people who have the necessary **engineering resources** to do an app's programming. Those who create apps tend to continue **iterating** an idea until they think it is ready for the market. It doesn't have to be the final version, but it has to reach the stage of being a **minimum viable product**. Only then are they ready to **launch**. Once they do, it's time to get people **jazzed** about it. This excitement can be generated through a **campaign**. In some cases, it helps to get a **blogger** to spread the news.

1. Silicon Valley (n.): ____

2. meet-ups (n.): ____

3. engineering resources (n.): ____

4. iterating (v.): ____

5. minimum viable product (n.): ____

6. launch (v.): ____

7. jazzed (adj.): ____

8. campaign (n.): ____

9. blogger (n.): ____

While You Listen

D. Watch a lecture by young entrepreneur Ben Silbermann. The first time you watch, try to understand the main idea. Listen for words that are repeated, words that point out parts that are more important, and changes in pitch and loudness. The lecture consists of eight sections. The first sentence or phrase of each section is numbered below. While you watch the second time, choose the best main idea for each section. Watch a third time to check the main ideas and make corrections.

1. Somebody asked me once, like, what's my big plan?
   a) His plan is to work for a large and successful software company.
   b) Pinterest is the speaker's goal for a useful product that others want to use.
   c) He would like to make something exciting and useful, like Pinterest.

2. We'd learned the lesson from doing the iPhone app ...
   a) There is no point in launching a product you are not proud of.
   b) It's better to launch a product early and get feedback to improve.
   c) It's difficult to launch a product on your own; work together.

3. And we decided that the one thing we had to do really well ...
   a) To succeed, the app needed to appeal to everyone.
   b) To succeed, the app had to be inexpensive.
   c) To succeed, the app had to be attractive.

4. So, this is the first version of Pinterest ...
   a) Creating the final app depended on countless small improvements.
   b) The initial app turned out to be much the same as the final product.
   c) The trial version of the app was thrown out and they started over.

5. I emailed out all my friends, like all my family ...
   a) It's better to change the product than find more users.
   b) It's better to find more users than change the product.
   c) Changing the product can help find more users.

6. And that's what we started to do ...
   a) By not having any strategy, we were able to let people choose.
   b) It was important to see which strategies were successful elsewhere.
   c) Finding a strategy appropriate to the app was important.

7. So it was a really, really exciting moment for us.
   a) The app avoided dividing people according to their interests.
   b) The best part of the app was connecting people with their shared interests.
   c) The unexpected part was that most people didn't want to meet others.

8. A lot of people in Silicon Valley didn't get it.
   a) The app included a virtual booklet to explain the app's special features.
   b) Others expected the app to have the same features as other apps.
   c) Once an app is launched, everyone expects it to do as well as other apps.

After You Listen

E. Indicate whether these statements are true or false, according to the video.

STATEMENTS	TRUE	FALSE
❶ Silbermann created Pinterest on his own.	☐	☑
❷ He wanted to create something that he would want to use.	☐	☐
❸ A new app has to have good features for you to get any feedback.	☐	☐
❹ Silbermann didn't show the app to anyone until it was launched.	☐	☐
❺ He tried to get his friends and family involved.	☐	☐
❻ Meet-ups were used to create a community of engineers.	☐	☐
❼ The word *genuine* is used to describe the connections that were made.	☐	☐
❽ It's important to listen to everyone else when designing a new app.	☐	☐

F. Now that you have identified the main idea for each section, what would you say is the main idea of the entire talk? Discuss this with a partner and then write the main idea below.

____

____

____

MyBookshelf > My eLab > Exercises > Chapter 1 > Ben Silbermann at Start-Up School

Academic
Survival Skill

Taking Notes

You take notes to help you remember the details of an assignment or lecture, or to have a record of a meeting so that you can bring up points and ask questions later. When your teacher offers additional explanations about something in your textbook, you can add notes to the particular section.

Taking notes helps to develop your listening skills. Learn to listen for main ideas and important details while blocking out information that doesn't matter. There are a number of ways to take notes including using mind maps, timelines, or outlines.

Mind Maps

Mind maps show relationships among ideas. Start with a central idea, such as the title of the lecture, and branch off to related ideas. In turn, the related ideas branch off further. If a topic changes, start a new mind map. One way to use a mind map is to write the topic in the centre circle with *who*, *what*, *when*, *where*, *why*, and *how* circles branching off from it.

A. Look at this example of a mind map summarizing Listening 2. Based on the mind map, discuss with a partner what you think Listening 2 is about.

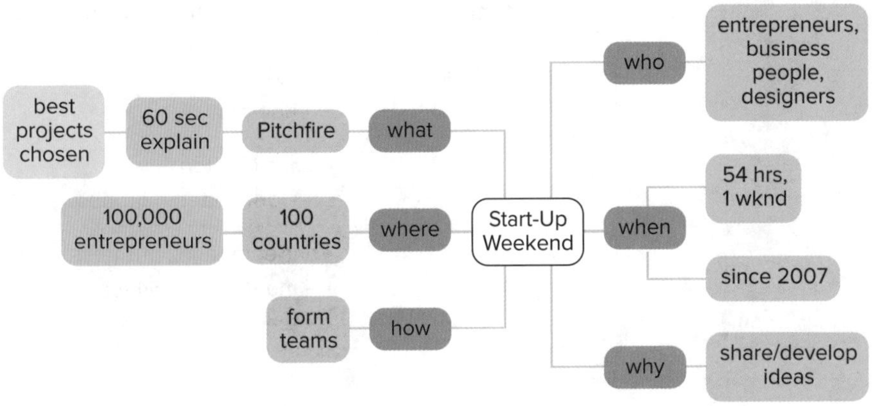

B. When you take notes, you don't have time to write everything the speaker says. Instead, write key words and use abbreviations and symbols: *sec*, *hrs*, and *wknd* for *seconds*, *hours*, and *weekend*. Write symbols you could use for the following terms.

MEANING	SYMBOL
greater than	>
less than	
equals/equal to	
not equal to	
connected ideas	
up/popular	
down/unpopular	

MEANING	SYMBOL
number	
dollars/money	
percent	
and/plus	
at	
essential information	or
not clear/question	

Timelines

When a lecture features several dates or refers to changes over time, take notes using a timeline. Draw a horizontal or vertical line on a page and add dates or stages. While you listen, write short notes next to each date or point in time.

C. Fill in the timeline with these short notes from Listening 1.

- meet-ups
- developed it with friends
- Pinterest success
- desire to design app
- S. wanted an app he could use
- showed friends, family

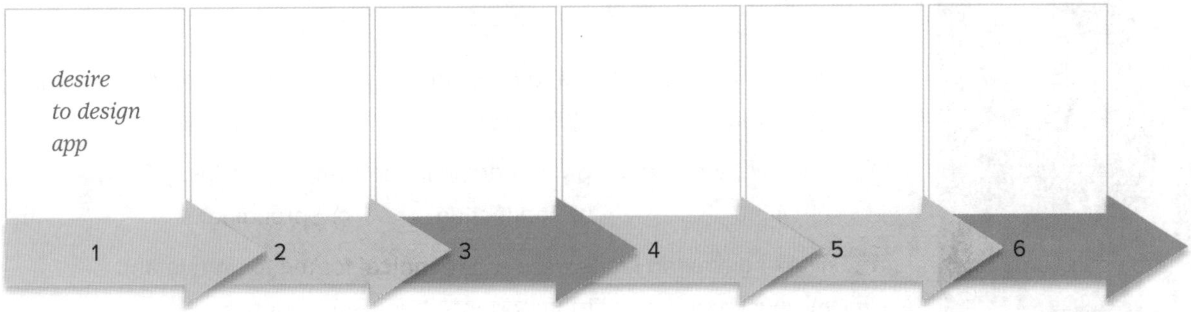

Outlines

Outlines work on the principle that main ideas are followed by supporting details. Look at this example. You will use this model to take notes on Listening 3.

Start-Up Weekend	• 2007 – non-profit
	• Isaac Newton – work better in groups
	• entrepreneurs, business people, designers – meet 1 wknd/54 hrs – teams, develop prototype

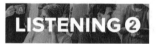

LISTENING 2 Fifty-Four Hours: Start-Up Weekend

Imagine you have a great idea for a new business but don't know anyone with the technical skills to help you make it happen. What would you do? Start-Up Weekend has been answering that question since 2007 with weekend get-togethers in more than one hundred countries. Participants share ideas and form teams to work on bringing the more interesting ideas closer to reality—all in just a fifty-four-hour period. In Listening 2, you will hear how some ideas might attract funding to get them started as real businesses.

VOCABULARY BUILD

In the following exercises, explore key words from Listening 2.

A. Highlight the word in parentheses that best completes each sentence. Key words are in bold.

1. I don't want to make a **commitment**, so I'll (choose / avoid) a date.
2. The new **facilitator** came to (organize / observe) the meeting.
3. The company has a special email **format** that (everyone / no one) must use.
4. The company preferred its **veterans**, not (older / newer) employees.
5. She wanted to do everything in **proportion** and (balance / unbalance) things.

B. Synonyms are words that have similar meanings. Choose the word or phrase that has the closest meaning to each word in bold.

1. One last **option** is to get money from a venture capitalist.
   a) decision b) dead end c) possibility
2. Wages were cut in half and **consequently** many people left the company.
   a) therefore b) beforehand c) unfortunately
3. They were **networking** with people in the computer industry.
   a) wiring b) connecting c) spreading
4. The engineering plans were too **technical** for me to understand.
   a) unusual b) important c) scientific

5. The software program tries to **simulate** the feeling of meeting friends in person.

   a) recover   b) imitate   c) introduce

C. VOCABULARY EXTENSION: Some words have both noun and verb forms. Write definitions for these words.

WORDS	NOUN DEFINITIONS	VERB DEFINITIONS
1 format	*way in which something is arranged*	
2 network		
3 option		
4 proportion		

D. Fill in the blanks with the words that have the closest meaning to the words and phrases in bold. These words will help you understand Listening 2.

circulate	incessantly	iterations	pitch	prototype	skits

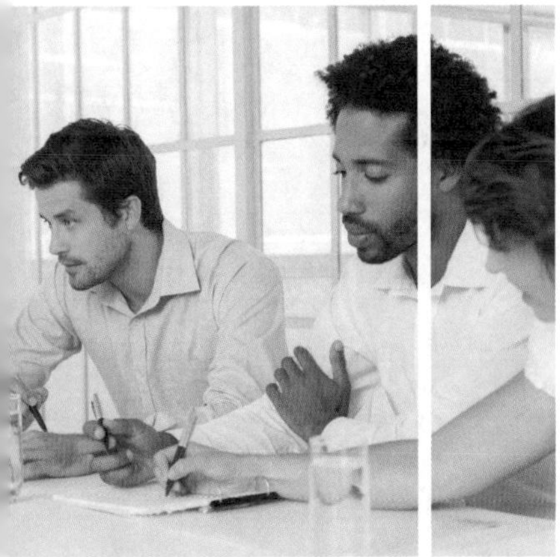

In funding meetings, **short performances** (____________) are often used as icebreakers to get people to **move around** (____________) and meet other people. If everyone moves **without stopping** (____________), however, then there won't be any time to make a **proposal** (____________). So there are **variations** (____________) of icebreakers, such as ones where you stand at a table with a **model** (____________) and people come to you.

Before You Listen

A. Form groups of six or more students. Ask each group member to write three or more skills he or she has, each one on a separate slip of paper. One member of the group collects and mixes these slips, then lays them out for everyone to see. In your group, look over the skills and make connections. Discuss how several skills could work together in a new business.

While You Listen

B. While you listen to the interview, try to focus on both the questions and the answers. On the next page are Jeff Smith's interview questions. Take notes on Louise Fox's answers. Then, when you finish listening, go back and add examples and explanations. Remember to use abbreviations when you take notes. You will hear the interview more than once, but take notes during the first time you listen, just as you might during a lecture.

SMITH'S QUESTIONS/COMMENTS	FOX'S ANSWERS/COMMENTS
1 Welcome, and today we're talking to Louise Fox who is working with Start-Up Weekend, an organization that's been around since 2004.	• *around since 2007*
2 ... It's sort of a meeting of geniuses and inventors, isn't it?	• *many innovations from groups* • *Isaac Newton agreed*
3 Did you say *giants*? What did he mean by giants?	
4 Got it! So tell us about Start-Up Weekend. Is it something that's going to change the world?	
5 Excuse me, just fifty-four? I heard that no one sleeps at these things!	
6 And I've heard it's been a success. Would you agree?	
7 Technical, design, business. Uh-huh.	• *Start-Up Weekend Friday night networking*
8 I've heard it's expensive to attend, but you said it was a non-profit. Can you tell me where all the money goes?	• *question not answered*
9 I understand that the teams are not just working on their own. Can you give me an example of the help they get?	• *coaches are Start-Up Weekend veterans*
10 Let me cut in here. It seems they're very motivated. What do you think?	
11 Would you be able to tell me what the presentations consist of?	• *presentations consist of*
12 Very impressive. For you, what would you say is the measure of success for Start-Up Weekend?	

After You Listen

C. Write short answers to these questions.

1. When did Start-Up Weekend first begin?

   ____

2. Why is the scientist Isaac Newton mentioned?

   ____

3. How many hours does Start-Up Weekend last?

   ____

4. What is the measure of the success for Start-Up Weekend?

   ____

5. What is the purpose of the Start-Up Weekend icebreaker activity?

   ____

6. Why do you think Pitchfire's time limit is only sixty seconds?

   ____

7. What is the purpose of the talks by experts?

   ____

8. What is the reason for the many formats used in the final presentations?

   ____

Isaac Newton (1643–1727) said he saw further by "standing on the shoulders of giants"—the scientists who came before him.

D. What would you expect to do at a Start-Up Weekend event? Number the following in order.

_______ ask for help from coaches

_______ form teams

___10___ listen for winners of top prototypes, and then celebrate and network

_______ listen to a short speech by the facilitator

___1___ network over dinner

_______ vote on best and most viable ideas

_______ prepare for a late-afternoon presentation and then respond to questions

_______ participate in an icebreaker

_______ share ideas in a Pitchfire session

_______ work together in teams, taking breaks to eat and drink

MyBookshelf > My eLab > Exercises > Chapter 1 > Fifty-Four Hours: Start-Up Weekend

E. Based on your notes and answers to task D, what is the main idea of Start-Up Weekend? Discuss in a group.

FOCUS ON SPEAKING

Managing a Conversation

Sometimes you are asked to listen without interrupting, such as in a lecture. Other times you are involved in the discussion and are expected to participate. An important part of participating is managing the conversation. These strategies can help improve your understanding of what is being said and allow you to contribute more effectively.

A. Read the strategies and practise the example conversation with a partner. Write phrases of your own in the empty squares in task B.

STRATEGIES	PURPOSE	EXAMPLE CONVERSATION
ASK FOR A RESPONSE	Make sure everyone is engaged in the conversation.	Do you agree? What's your opinion? What do you think?
ASK FOR MORE DETAIL	Find out more information.	Could you explain that? How exactly does that work?
ASK FOR CLARIFICATION	Find out the meaning of a word or other detail.	So you're saying that ... Let me get this straight ... I'm not sure what you mean by ... Are you sure?
EXPRESS AN OPINION	Share an idea, even though it may not be supported by facts.	I don't agree. That seems wrong. That doesn't seem right to me.
POLITELY INTERRUPT	Make space in the conversation for your questions or point of view.	Excuse me, but my point is ... Before you go on, could I add ... Please, let me say something here.

See Appendix 1 (page 187) for additional ways to manage a conversation.

B. In a small group, discuss which of your courses will most likely help you get a job. During the conversation, try to use each strategy at least once. Keep your book open to this page, and, when a group member uses one of the strategies, check its box.

ask for a response		ask for more detail	
ask for clarification	express an opinion		politely interrupt

Pronunciation: To improve your pronunciation, record what you hear; then, record yourself repeating it and compare the two.

MyBookshelf > My eLab > Exercises > Chapter 1 > Focus on Speaking

C. With your group, discuss which strategies were used more often and which strategies were seldom used, and why.

FOCUS ON GRAMMAR

Yes/No Questions

You have already seen questions that ask *who*, *what*, *when*, *where*, *why*, and *how*. These types of questions are called information questions. Information questions ask for information by using question words that encourage short specific answers. But, when you want the briefest answer possible, ask questions that have *yes* or *no* answers.

VERB *to be*	SUBJECT	PHRASE	ANSWERS
Are Aren't	you	networking?	Yes, I am (networking). No, I'm not (networking).
Is Isn't	she	Louise Fox?	Yes, she is (Louise Fox). No, she's not (Louise Fox).
Am Aren't	I	late?	Yes, you are (late). No, you aren't (late).
VERB *to do*	**SUBJECT**	**PHRASE**	**ANSWERS**
Do Don't	you	know Louise?	Yes, I do (know Louise). No, I don't (know Louise).
Does Doesn't	he	network?	Yes, he does (network). No, he doesn't (network).
Did Didn't	they	finish?	Yes, they did (finish). No, they didn't (finish).
VERB *to have*	**SUBJECT**	**PHRASE**	**ANSWERS**
Has Hasn't	he	networked?	Yes, he has (networked). No, he hasn't (networked).
Have Haven't	you	met Louise?	Yes, I have (met Louise). No, I haven't (met Louise).
Has Hasn't	the group	finished?	Yes, the group has (finished). No, the group hasn't (finished).

!

When people speak quickly, they often blend the final sound of one word together with the first sound of another. Listen carefully to understand the individual words.

A. Change these information questions to *yes* or *no* questions.

1. Who offers the workshops?

____

2. What has made your company more efficient?

____

3. When did you start your company?

____

Use what you learned about yes/no questions when you prepare assignments.

④ Where is your company located?

____

⑤ Why did you start a company?

____

⑥ How do people volunteer with you?

____

MyBookshelf > My eLab > Exercises > Chapter 1 > Grammar Review

B. Practise asking and answering the questions with a partner.

WARM-UP ASSIGNMENT

Work in a Group to Create an Idea for an Application

In this Warm-Up Assignment, you will work in groups to create an idea for a new digital application.

The following are among the most popular applications downloaded for smartphones.

- banking
- communication
- entertainment
- food
- games
- maps
- music
- news
- productivity
- shopping
- social networking
- sports
- travel
- video
- weather

A. Form groups of three. From the list above, work together to combine two or more of the applications to create an idea for a new one. For example, you might combine *social networking* + *banking* to compete with friends on ways to save money, or you might combine *weather* + *maps* + *entertainment* to play a game to learn about different kinds of clouds.

B. Discuss your ideas. Use the conversation strategies you learned in Focus on Speaking (page 16). Ask questions about different applications and how they work (refer to Focus on Grammar).

C. Make notes to explain how

- the idea came about;
- the application works;
- the application could solve a problem;
- the application could be used to learn something new.

D. Share your ideas and ask for feedback from your teacher and classmates. Use this feedback to prepare for your presentation during the Final Assignment.

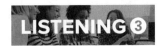

LISTENING 3

Start-Up and Slay

The phrase *glass ceiling* refers to the barriers in the workplace that stop some women and minorities from getting ahead. It's as if one cannot move to higher and more important floors and jobs in an office building. Start-ups provide opportunities for many different people to move ahead in business, especially if they start it themselves. This is especially true for young people. But, to get started, it helps to network, as described in Listening 3.

VOCABULARY BUILD

In the following exercises, explore key words from Listening 3.

A. Choose the phrase that best completes each sentence. Key words are in bold.

1. He clearly wanted the **status quo**, that, is for _______.
   a) nothing to change
   b) only limited changes
   c) everything to change
2. The **demographic** groups generally interested in start-ups_______.
   a) tend to be younger
   b) are large cities
   c) include companies
3. The team's **tenacity** meant they _______.
   a) gave up too easily
   b) were realistic
   c) never gave up
4. In looking for **diversity** on the team, they tried to find _______.
   a) the same qualifications
   b) shared backgrounds
   c) a variety of backgrounds
5. There was little **tangible** information about the project, _______.
   a) only wishful thinking
   b) it filled several books
   c) only visual information

B. Highlight the word or phrase that has the closest meaning to each word in bold.

1. We have all had our failures and our **triumphs**.
   a) losses b) wins c) ties
2. Once unique, computer science backgrounds are now **prevalent**.
   a) common b) unnecessary c) uncommon

3. In asking for **transparency**, the team wanted to better understand the decisions.

a) invisibility b) changes c) openness

4. As a **consumer**, he wants to ensure he gets the best deals.

a) buyer b) payee c) enrolee

5. Her **presence** in the office encouraged the whole team to do its best.

a) absence b) questioning c) being around

MyBookshelf > My eLab > Exercises > Chapter 1 > Vocabulary Review

Before You Listen

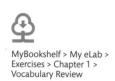

A. Read an excerpt from Listening 3. Based on the excerpt, and on the title and the introduction, which questions would you expect to have answered? Write the questions and the answers.

> **Host:** Tonight, six women will gather at Spaces on John Street to share their stories, triumphs, and tips for launching start-ups. It's all part of Start-Up and Slay, a new information and networking event featuring diverse female entrepreneurs. Eva Wong is one of the people taking part. She is co-founder and chief operating officer of Borrowell, a credit score and personal loan company here in Toronto. And she is with me in studio. Eva, good morning.

1. Who *is Eva Wong?*

She is co-founder and chief operating officer of Borrowell.

2. What ______

3. When ______

4. Where ______

5. Why ______

B. In the introduction, the host explains that the event is for women only. Why might women be more interested in having the workshops for women rather than in a mixed group of women and men?

______

While You Listen

C. The first time you listen, try to get the main idea. Listen a second time for key words. Use the outline technique from Academic Survival Skill (page 10) to take notes. Listen a third time to check your notes and add details.

HOST: And now, you're running a company that raised, what, $60 million in funding last year? ... How does that happen?

- a twenty-year-old college dropout can start a successful company
- ______
- ______

HOST: How did this all start for you?

- a group wanted to challenge consumer-debt problem
- ______
- ______

HOST: How long was that process?

- four years

HOST: Yeah? And along that process, what were some of the things that stood out to you in terms of, oh, "I didn't know that we'd be getting involved in this?" ... Or "This is actually more rewarding than I might have expected"?

- more rewarding than expected
- ______
- ______

HOST: I was going to say, How do you go about building trust if people already have trust in these enormous organizations? ... Why should they trust you if this giant thing over here ... is the place that I've been going to forever?

- media helped
- ______
- ______
- ______

HOST: Does it help, then, if you are a bit of an outsider in this industry?

- ______
- ______

HOST: And were people willing to give it up and kind of offer advice and mentorship and bring you along in that?

- Start-up community in Toronto supportive
- ______

HOST: Can you go back to what you started out talking to us about, which is the assumptions that we make as a society about who is going to be an innovator and who is not going to be an innovator? ... How prevalent are those assumptions?

- prevalent
- example of being considered an assistant
- ______
- ______

▶

HOST: Have you been able to influence diversity at your workplace? Something that we've talked a lot about on the program ... as an issue within start-ups?

- yes, since the beginning
- ______
- ______
- ______
- ______
- ______
- ______
- ______

After You Listen

D. Based on the notes you took, what are the advantages and disadvantages in creating a start-up? Write two points for each, and share in a group to pick the best ones.

ADVANTAGES: ______

DISADVANTAGES: ______

E. Highlight the word or phrase in parentheses that best completes each sentence.

1. Eva Wong is a (company co-founder / stay-at-home mom).
2. Last year her company raised (awareness among start-ups / $60 million).
3. The consumer-debt problem is about a lack of (credit scores / transparency).
4. One challenge is (building / measuring) consumer trust.
5. The idea of giving people something is (less / more) successful if you don't ask too much in return.
6. In terms of the status quo, Wong wants to (change / maintain) it.
7. One problem Wong faces is being mistaken as (a co-founder / an executive assistant).
8. In the company, a higher percentage of people are (women / management).

F. Choose the sentence that best expresses the main idea of Listening 3.

☐ Eva Wong is a success in the credit and financial industry.

☐ Women in start-ups can achieve more by working together

☐ It's good business to take advantage of people's credit score.

MyBookshelf > My eLab > Exercises > Chapter 1 > Start-Up and Slay

FINAL ASSIGNMENT

Give a Presentation and Take Notes

Use what you learned in this chapter to deliver a presentation based on your ideas in the Warm-Up Assignment. You will also take notes on the presentations of other groups.

A. Re-form your Warm-Up Assignment group.

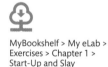

B. Based on the feedback you received from your teacher and classmates, consider how you can improve your Warm-Up Assignment application and presentation. Make revisions.

C. Divide the presentation among group members. Each group member might be responsible for one of the following:

- how the idea came about;
- how the application works;
- how the application could solve a problem;
- how the application could be used to learn something new.

D. While you listen to your classmates' presentations, take notes using symbols and a mind map, a timeline, or an outline format (see Academic Survival Skill, page 10).

E. While you listen, write your feedback questions, comments, and suggestions. Depending on the response you need, ask either yes/no questions or information questions with *who*, *what*, *when*, *where*, *why*, and *how* question words (Focus on Grammar, page 17). If you need to interrupt a presentation, do so politely.

F. When all the presentations are finished, as a class, vote for the best application. A group cannot vote for its own application.

How confident are you?

Think about what you learned in this chapter. Use the table to decide what you should review.

I LEARNED ...	I AM CONFIDENT	I NEED TO REVIEW
vocabulary related to new business models;	☐	☐
to listen for the main idea;	☐	☐
to identify advantages and disadvantages;	☐	☐
how to organize ideas using note-taking strategies;	☐	☐
to manage conversations;	☐	☐
about yes/no questions;	☐	☐
to work in a group to create an idea for an app;	☐	☐
how to give a presentation and take notes.	☐	☐

CHAPTER 2

A New World of Work

The question, "What do you want to do when you grow up?" is one you probably heard as a child but, as you grow older, is increasingly difficult to answer. In past centuries, children often trained to take over the occupations of their parents, who, in turn, had been taught by their parents. Education has since broadened the job options for most young people, but it can be difficult to choose subjects to study and, after, to choose a career.

What is your perfect job, and how can you get it?

In this chapter, you will

- learn vocabulary related to future work;
- listen for compare and contrast;
- use active listening strategies;
- review comparative and superlative adjectives;
- use intonation and stress;
- give a descriptive presentation;
- learn compare and contrast presentation structure;
- learn about citations and references in presentations;
- give a compare and contrast presentation with a partner.

GEARING UP

A. Look at the diagram and then answer the questions.

Predicted shortages and surpluses for university graduates in the workplace

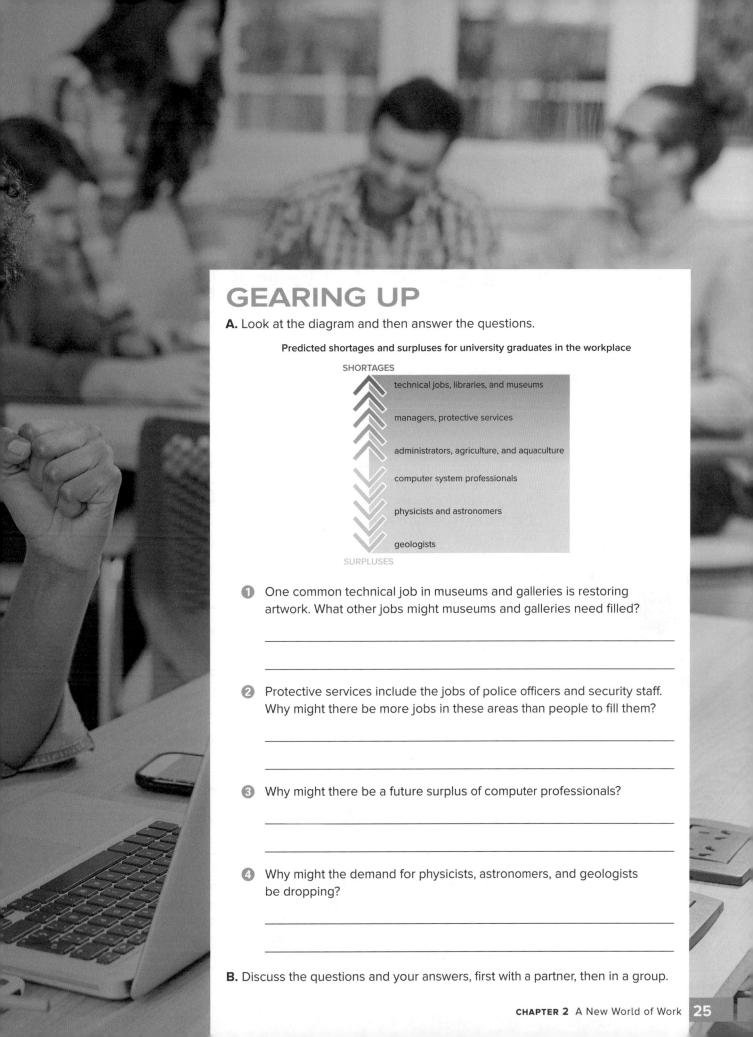

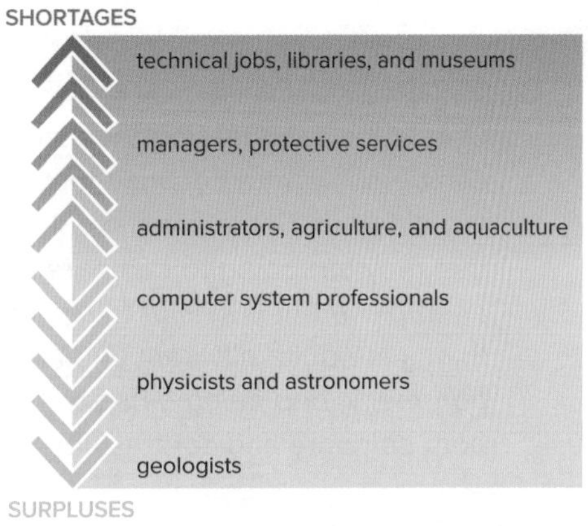

1. One common technical job in museums and galleries is restoring artwork. What other jobs might museums and galleries need filled?

   ____

   ____

2. Protective services include the jobs of police officers and security staff. Why might there be more jobs in these areas than people to fill them?

   ____

   ____

3. Why might there be a future surplus of computer professionals?

   ____

   ____

4. Why might the demand for physicists, astronomers, and geologists be dropping?

   ____

   ____

B. Discuss the questions and your answers, first with a partner, then in a group.

VOCABULARY BUILD OVERVIEW

Below are the key words you will practise in this chapter. Check the words you understand, then underline the words you use. Highlight the words you need to learn.

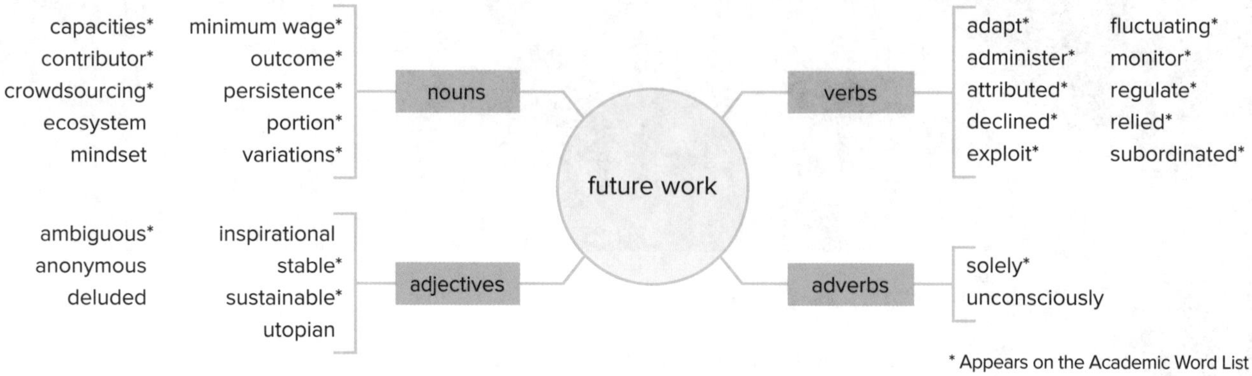

* Appears on the Academic Word List

FOCUS ON LISTENING

Listening for Compare and Contrast

One of the most natural things for you to do is to look and listen for things that can be compared because they are similar, or that are contrasted because they are different. Sometimes speakers introduce a topic in a way that makes it clear that they are going to compare two topics—for example, *I'd like to show how unemployment is similar to retirement*. Or a speaker may make it clear that two things are quite different and are contrasted: *I'd like to explain why being a paramedic and being a nurse can be quite different occupations*. Often, speakers both compare and contrast the same topic.

A. The following phrases show comparison and contrast. Highlight the ones that show comparison.

- as well as
- both
- but
- by the same token
- however
- in comparison
- in contrast
- in similar fashion
- in the same manner
- in the same way
- likewise
- nevertheless
- on the contrary
- on the other hand
- otherwise
- similarly
- though
- yet

When you listen for comparisons and contrasts, a good note-taking strategy is to use a Venn diagram of two or more overlapping circles. The overlapping portion shows what can be compared as being similar, and the segments on either side show how two things are unique, or contrast, in some way.

B. Read the paragraph and fill in the Venn diagram with comparisons and contrasts.

> Two jobs that are sometimes confused are *computer programmer* and *web designer*. While both jobs involve working with computers and require coding, web designers do not generally work on non-web coding projects like apps and security systems. Programmers do not generally worry about visual appeal in their work. Both professions need to keep up with the latest developments in operating systems.

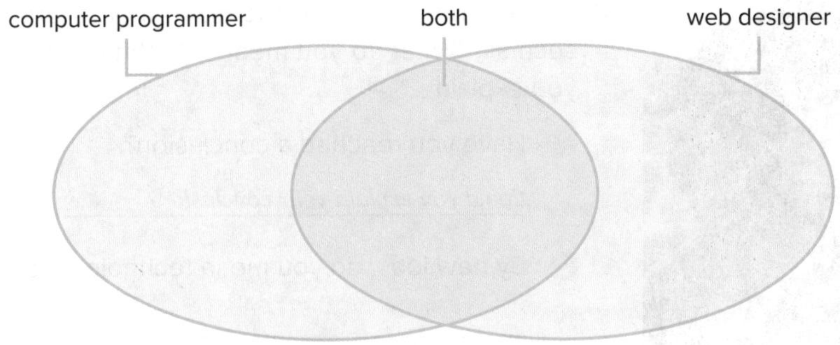

FOCUS ON CRITICAL THINKING

Using Active Listening Strategies

When you listen, whether it is to a formal lecture or a casual conversation, you need to listen actively. Active listening means focused listening: paying close attention to what is being said and showing that you are listening.

A. What purposes do you have when you listen to lectures and take part in conversations? Discuss with a partner.

B. Here are some strategies you can use to actively listen. For each, indicate whether it would be more appropriate to use when listening to a lecture or to a conversation, or both.

LISTENING STRATEGIES	LECTURE	CONVERSATION	BOTH
1 Make eye contact and use non-verbal body language to show you're interested in what the speaker has to say.	☐	☐	☐
2 Listen patiently, but interrupt to ask questions when you do not understand.	☐	☐	☐
3 Listen for ways in which the speaker's ideas fit or conflict with your own.	☐	☐	☐
4 Avoid distractions; ensure that your phone and other devices are set to silent.	☐	☐	☐
5 Take notes and paraphrase and summarize what the speaker says.	☐	☐	☐
6 Give the speaker the benefit of the doubt, not rejecting anything that is said until all ideas are explained in full.	☐	☐	☐
7 Interact with the speaker with sounds or body language that show you agree or disagree, or that you are confused.	☐	☐	☐
8 After, reflect on what you have heard and modify your ideas or notes, adding your own interpretations of what has been said.	☐	☐	☐

Active listening often involves asking questions to clarify. Sometimes you ask closed-ended questions to get a *yes* or *no* answer. Other times, you ask open-ended questions that encourage the speaker to share more.

C. Rewrite these questions to make them more open-ended. Use phrases such as, "What do you mean ...," "What makes you think ...," and "Could you explain ..."

1. Have you reached a conclusion?

   Could you explain your conclusion?

2. By new jobs, do you mean technology jobs?

   ____

3. Nobody believes there will be 50 percent unemployment, do they?

   ____

4. Everyone knows cashier jobs are on the way out, right?

   ____

5. So, are you saying that it would be foolish to work in heavy industry?

   ____

LISTENING 1

Don't Follow Your Passion

Part of growing up is having to make more and more difficult decisions. These decisions become harder because each one might have long-lasting impacts on your life. One of the biggest decisions is deciding what you might want to do for a career. Some people know from a young age. Other people take time—and several changes of jobs—to discover what they really want to do.

VOCABULARY BUILD

In the following exercises, explore key words from Listening 1.

A. Highlight the word or phrase in parentheses that best completes each sentence. Key words are in bold.

1. **Variations** in interests mean different people will enjoy (different / the same) jobs.
2. These variations can sometimes be **attributed** to the way you were (lowered / raised), or influences from peers or family members.
3. If you are not sure about what you want to do, a counsellor will **administer** a (medicine / test) to see what skills you have.
4. But these can be **ambiguous** because, even if you're good at something, it doesn't mean you (dislike / enjoy) it.
5. Moreover, as you get older, you may find your interests **fluctuating** as you (encounter / reject) new ideas and opportunities.

B. Fill in the blanks with the correct words to complete the sentences

anonymous	inspirational	mindset	subordinated	unconsciously

1. Many people find that their dreams are __________________ when they have to choose a job that earns more.
2. They may find it __________________ that other people have achieved their dreams later in life.
3. But for all these well-known achievers, there are many __________________ people who did not encounter personal success.
4. However, either deliberately or __________________, it's important to never stop trying.
5. It's the only __________________ that will allow you to reach for your dreams.

Before You Listen

A. What is something you feel passionate about? Could you find a job that makes use of that passion? Why or why not? Discuss your answers in a group.

B. Read the following excerpt from Listening 1. What do you think is meant by the terms *fixed interest mindset* and *growth mindset*? Discuss your answers with a partner, and check back after you have finished listening.

> ... focusing on a single passion might get in the way of finding work that is, in many ways, [...] more rewarding. Moreover, there's a strong alternative to choosing a job tied to your passion. Yale psychologist Paul O'Keefe and Stanford University psychologists Carol Dweck and Gregory Walton have done experiments with students to explore the differences. They define the two alternatives as a *fixed interest mindset* that can be contrasted with a *growth mindset*.

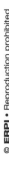

! A speaker may say "compare" but still point out contrasts.

- A FIXED INTEREST MINDSET MEANS: __________________
- A GROWTH MINDSET MEANS: __________________

While You Listen

C. Listen once and identify points about the fixed interest mindset. Listen again and identify contrasting points about the growth mindset. Listen a third time to see what the two mindsets have in common.

A FIXED INTEREST MINDSET	BOTH	A GROWTH MINDSET
passion for your job		

A FIXED INTEREST MINDSET	BOTH	A GROWTH MINDSET

After You Listen

D. Indicate whether each statement is true or false, according to the listening. For those that are false, write the correct statement.

STATEMENTS	TRUE	FALSE
1 Advice about following your passion is common.	☐	☐
2 The article mentions following your passion as the best way to earn money.	☐	☐
3 This *passion-equals-happiness* advice was first written by Confucius.	☐	☐
4 Experiments with teachers explored the differences between a fixed interest mindset and a growth mindset.	☐	☐
5 Many people's passions are also things for which they have great talents.	☐	☐
6 The speaker was aware of his interest in psychology as early as kindergarten.	☐	☐
7 A growth mindset provides more opportunities to learn new ideas and skills.	☐	☐
8 The speaker studied engineering because it was his first passion.	☐	☐
9 The speaker's hobbies led to his interest in teaching.	☐	☐
10 Experiencing the world and learning from it might help some discover their passions.	☐	☐

E. People often ignore their passions because they don't think there are practical jobs that can make use of those passions. For each passion, write three jobs that closely relate.

- MUSIC: ____________________
- NATURE: ____________________
- TRAVEL: ____________________

MyBookshelf > My eLab > Exercises > Chapter 2 > Don't Follow Your Passion

F. Do you think you have more of a *fixed interest mindset* or a *growth mindset*? Why? After the listening, would you consider changing your mindset? Why or why not? Discuss in a group.

FOCUS ON GRAMMAR

Comparative and Superlative Form

In Listening 1, you heard phrases like "my older self" and "the most dangerous jobs." Adjectives (e.g., *old*, *dangerous*) describe nouns, and adverbs describe verbs. Comparatives (e.g., *older*, *more dangerous*) compare two nouns or verbs, saying which is more or less than the other. Superlatives (e.g., *oldest*, *most dangerous*) describe nouns or verbs as being the most or least of three or more things.

A. Read the rules for how to form comparative and superlative adjectives. Then, choose other words to write new examples.

RULES	COMPARATIVE	SUPERLATIVE
for one-syllable adjectives ending in *-e* EXAMPLE: safe	add *-r* + *than* safe**r than** ________	put *the* before the adjective and add *-st* **the** safe**st** ________
for one-syllable adjectives ending in a consonant EXAMPLE: hot	double the consonant and add *-er* + *than* hot**ter than** ________	put *the* before the adjective, double the consonant, and add *-est* **the** hot**test** ________
for two-syllable adjectives ending in *-y* EXAMPLE: happy	change the *y* to *i* and add *-er* + *than* happ**ier than** ________	put *the* before the adjective, change *y* to *i*, and add *-est* **the** happ**iest** ________
for two or more syllables not ending in *-y* EXAMPLE: realistic	put *more* before and *than* after the adjective **more** realistic **than** ________	put *the most* before the adjective **the most** realistic ________

B. Some adjectives have irregular forms of comparatives and superlatives. They are exceptions to the rules. You need to memorize them. Fill in the missing words.

ADJECTIVES	COMPARATIVE	SUPERLATIVE
________	worse	worst
good	________	best
________	less	least
much	________	most
far	farther (distance) / further (time)	________ (distance) / (time)

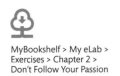

C. Change the adjective in parentheses to either the comparative or the superlative form.

1. He had the (good, superlative) ____________________ reason for finishing his degree.
2. We had the (fine, superlative) ____________________ interns working for the new company.
3. Their new jobs were (interesting, comparative) ____________________ ____________________ than their old ones.
4. She told me to put (little, comparative) ____________________ emphasis on looking for a job.
5. Technology start-ups tend to feature the (trendy, superlative) ____________________ jobs.
6. Some interns were (busy, comparative) ____________________ than others.

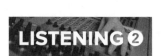

Use what you learned about comparatives and superlatives when you prepare assignments.

MyBookshelf > My eLab > Exercises > Chapter 2 > Grammar Review

LISTENING 2 VIDEO

Students Create Their Own Dream Jobs

A new approach to developing businesses is the *innovation incubator*. It is based on inviting individuals or groups to bring new business ideas to a group of experienced mentors (advisors) who can help develop the ideas. Often, part of this process includes competition: the individuals or groups with the best ideas get funding. This format has become common in the business world as well as on TV. In Listening 2, you will hear how a version of this approach is being used at a college.

VOCABULARY BUILD

In the following exercises, explore key words from Listening 2.

A. Highlight the word or phrase that has the closest meaning to each word or phrase in bold.

1. Her **persistence** in practising day after day paid off with a gold medal.
   a) savings b) determination c) relaxed attitude
2. He took only a small **portion** of the food, knowing that others would want some.
   a) share b) investment c) total
3. I have always **relied on** the kindness of strangers.
   a) regretted b) trusted in c) been cautious about
4. Each of us lives in an **ecosystem** with other living things.
   a) recycling b) self-interest c) network

B. Fill in the blanks with the correct words to complete the paragraph.

adapt	deluded	capacities	solely	sustainable

People are ______________________ if they think universities can ______________________ focus on doing things the way they've always been done. A key concept in many universities is the idea of making things ______________________. This is done by looking at ways to ensure that the university can ______________________ to future challenges. To function at their peak ______________________, universities must attract new students, retain old ones, and prepare them all for life beyond university.

C. VOCABULARY EXTENSION: The suffix *-able* turns some verbs into adjectives. Change these verbs into adjectives by adding *-able*. If the verb ends in *-y*, change the *y* to *i*; if the verb ends in *-e*, drop the *e*.

VERBS	ADJECTIVES
1 adapt	
2 compare	
3 deplore	
4 like	

VERBS	ADJECTIVES
5 rely	
6 note	
7 vary	
8 prefer	

Before You Listen

A. One of the proposed businesses in Listening 2 is a motivational musician's plan to make money by charging for appearances at schools. If you were a mentor, what questions would you have about this kind of business? Write four questions and then discuss them with a partner.

1. ____
2. ____
3. ____
4. ____

B. Read this excerpt from Listening 2. In it, the narrator describes the motivation for students to become involved in the innovation incubator. Why might students prefer to create their dream jobs rather than wait to apply for them?

> With media students producing it, Humber College's LaunchPad Competition is a live test of nerves: an innovation incubator where current students and recent grads compete for cash to finance their own businesses. Some have already tested out the job market, but no one here has found their dream job or is willing to wait for it. They want to create it.

____

____

hydroponics

C. These words in bold will help you understand Listening 2. Highlight the word or phrase in parentheses that best completes the sentence.

1. **Aquaculture**, farming fish and other sea life, is a (limited / sustainable practice).
2. **Hydroponics** involves growing plants without (soil / water).
3. There was a **looming** deadline that meant they had (to finish quickly / lots of time).
4. A **nutrient-based** product was used to (take away / add to) the plants' food.
5. The company **preps** its employees so they (are ready / don't have) to make sales.

While You Listen

D. The first time you watch, try to understand the general idea. Before you watch a second time, read the following questions. While you watch the second time, take notes on a separate page to help you answer the questions. Answer the questions, then watch a third time to check your answers and fill in details.

1. When the first woman says that the unemployment rate among recent graduates is "pretty dismal," what does she mean?

   ____

2. What is one problem with the job market?

   ____

3. Craig Petten and Pablo Alvarez have jobs. Why are they anxious to change?

   ____

4. Why do Lindsay Branton and Brennon Lundy want to start their own business?

   ____

5. What is unusual about artist Colin Edwards's job idea?

   ____

6. What is the reason for competitions that ask students to do things like come up with a social media plan?

   ____

7. At the Humber innovation incubator, what is the role of the panel of judges?

   ____

8. How much were Lindsay and Brennon asking for, and how much did they get?

   ____

9. Which group won the competition, and how much did they get?

____

After You Listen

E. Write the details of the businesses associated with the following people.

1. Craig Petten and Pablo Alvarez: ____
2. Lindsay Branton and Brennon Lundy: ____
3. Colin Edwards: ____
4. Lauren Friese: ____

F. Answer these questions. With a partner, discuss what each answer might mean to you.

1. Why does the narrator use the words *dreamers, risk-takers*, and *optimists* to describe the students?

   ____

   What it means to me: ____

2. Why is this generation different?

   ____

   What it means to me: ____

3. Why is entrepreneurship risky?

   ____

   What it means to me: ____

4. What is the importance of learning to compete in business?

   ____

   What it means to me: ____

Pronunciation: As you gather your thoughts or think of how to pronounce a word, try to avoid filling the pause with "um" or "ah." It's better to look away for a moment.

5. Why does Friese mention the idea of standing out?

____

____

What it means to me: ______________________________

____

6. Why is persistence important?

____

____

What it means to me: ______________________________

____

____

MyBookshelf > My eLab > Exercises > Chapter 2 > Students Create Their Own Dream Jobs

FOCUS ON SPEAKING

Using Intonation and Stress

When you speak, it's important to add intonation and stress to your words and sentences. *Intonation* refers to the rise and fall of your voice as you speak. For example, when you ask a question, your voice usually rises on the last word. *Stress* refers to the emphasis you put on different parts (syllables) of words. Sometimes stress on different syllables changes the meaning of a word, such as the noun *sub*ject and the verb sub*ject*.

A. Write a second sentence for the verb form of each word. The stress falls on the first syllable for the noun form and on the second syllable for the verb form. Practise saying each sentence with a partner.

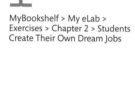

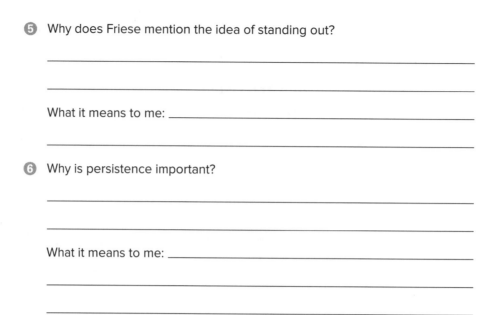

1. address (n.): The address is on Broadway.

   address (v.): ______________________________

2. conduct (n.): The conduct of the team was excellent.

   conduct (v.): ______________________________

3. conflict (n.): The war zone conflict is increasing.

   conflict (v.): ______________________________

4. decrease (n.): We saw a decrease in waste.

   decrease (v.): ______________________________

5. permit (n.): I have a permit to build the house.

   permit (v.): ______________________________

6. record (n.): The record shows that she is innocent.

   record (v.): ______________________________

B. Punctuation signals changes in intonation. Commas, semicolons, and colons signal short pauses, and periods signal longer pauses. Practise saying these sentences with a partner.

- Every job, I think, has someone who would love to fill it.
- Here's an idea: Everyone can have a perfect job.
- Thinking a moment, he asked, "What would be different?"
- So, the coolest thing is you can choose what you want, can't you?
- It's good to schedule ten or fifteen minutes, every day, as a time to think.

MyBookshelf > My eLab > Exercises > Chapter 2 > Focus on Speaking

WARM-UP ASSIGNMENT

Describe Your Perfect Job

Listening 1 explained two mindsets that influence the jobs you seek, and Listening 2 focused on creating your own dream job. In this Warm-Up Assignment, you will give a presentation of less than five minutes describing your perfect job.

A. Begin by choosing your topic. Consider some of the factors that would make a job perfect for you: the kind of skills needed, the hours and duties required, the working conditions, and the amount of pay expected. Ask your teacher to approve your choice.

B. Write an outline of your presentation. When you explain why your job is the best or what makes your perfect job better than other jobs, use comparative and superlative adjectives (see Focus on Grammar, page 31). For example,

> Being an astronaut is **better than** being a pilot because your trips can last for weeks, not hours. **The greatest** thing about being an astronaut is having a view of the world that few experience.

C. Practise your presentation on your own and with a partner. Then, present to the class. You can use key words to help you present, but do not read from your notes. Make eye contact and use body language to show your enthusiasm for your topic. When you speak, use what you learned in Focus on Speaking to vary your intonation and stress.

D. While you listen to other students' presentations, use the active listening strategies you learned in Focus on Listening (page 26): ask questions and take notes so that you will be prepared to give feedback.

E. Once everyone has presented, ask for feedback from your teacher and classmates on how you could improve your presentation.

Visit My eLab Documents for suggestions on effective presentations.

LISTENING 3

Crowdworkers

In 1770, a chess-playing robot called the Mechanical Turk became a popular attraction in Europe. The robot, placed at a chess table, would play a game against skillful players and usually win. However, it was later shown to be a hoax: an expert human player hid inside the machine. The term *mechanical turk* or *m-turk* is now used for workers who work online completing small writing and programming tasks. In Listening 3, mechanical turks (turkers) are interviewed to find out about the advantages and disadvantages of their jobs.

VOCABULARY BUILD

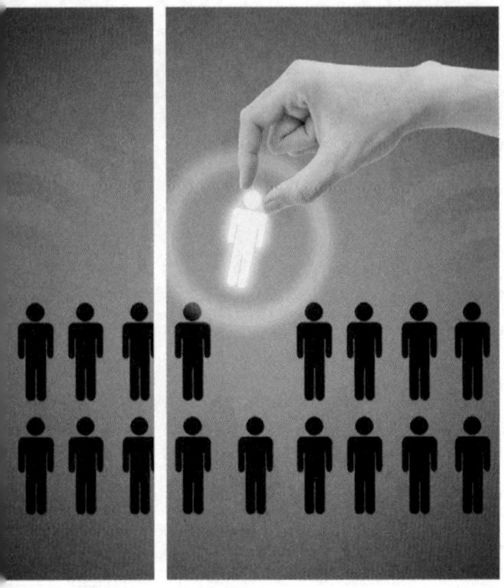

In the following exercises, explore key words from Listening 3.

A. Choose the phrase that best completes each sentence. Key words are in bold.

1. The **contributor** to the magazine ________.
   a) delivered copies to the store
   b) wrote articles for publication
   c) performed editorial duties

2. Many people want a **stable** job that ________.
   a) they may only do for a short time
   b) is a kind of seasonal employment
   c) stays the same year after year

3. The principle of a **minimum wage** is ________.
   a) to ensure that workers can afford to live
   b) so employers do not have to pay extra
   c) to avoid paying what is naturally fair

4. Businesses use **crowdsourcing** when they need ________.
   a) permanent staff to work on ideas
   b) to find one or two select employees
   c) many people helping with a project

5. The idea of creating a **utopian** society was ________.
   a) to take away workers' rights
   b) to make everyone's job perfect
   c) to reduce wasted resources

B. Choose the best definition for each key word in bold. Use a dictionary to check your answers.

1	**regulate**	a) give up on something	b) control or supervise something
2	**monitor**	a) observe a process or activity	b) plan to review activities
3	**outcome**	a) result	b) preparation
4	**declined**	a) accepted	b) refused
5	**exploit**	a) fully use to your advantage	b) have an individual adventure

MyBookshelf > My eLab > Exercises > Chapter 2 > Vocabulary Review

Before You Listen

A. Google's chief executive officer Larry Page believes that the future of employment—for everyone—will be part-time. Many of us will have jobs that can be done online and will allow us to work from different locations for short periods of time. With a partner, discuss jobs that could fit this new model. Talk about other jobs that would not fit the model.

B. The opening paragraph of Listening 3 points out the issue of questionable labour practices. What problems might there be, in terms of pay and working conditions, for individuals working online doing mini-tasks?

> The Internet makes it easier for an individual to work at home, but it goes beyond that. Now, businesses can break down an individual's job into fragmented mini-tasks that can be done by many people scattered all over the world. And the explosion of this crowdsourced online micro-work has led to some questionable labour practices.

____

____

____

____

C. It's sometimes difficult to know the meaning of a phrase from its individual words. These phrases are important for your understanding of Listening 3. Choose the best definition for each. Use a dictionary to look up those that are unfamiliar.

1	grizzly details	a) unpleasant facts	b) bare necessities
2	decent living	a) proper behaviour	b) having enough to live on
3	enviable lifestyle	a) being always jealous	b) kind of life others want
4	legitimate way	a) workable solution	b) illegal move
5	class actions	a) group legal cases	b) strikes by students
6	green light	a) traffic warning	b) permission to proceed
7	industrial revolution	a) machine labour	b) robot attack
8	tide me over	a) overcome by waves	b) have enough to survive temporarily

While You Listen

D. The first time you listen, try to get the general idea. Listen a second time and take notes on each segment. Focus on the main message and consider whether the explanations and examples support the speakers' main ideas. Listen a third time to check your notes and add details.

SEGMENTS	NOTES
Working flexible hours anywhere with a Wi-Fi connection	
Bateman avoids some crowdsourcing platforms.	

SEGMENTS	NOTES
Mechanical Turk is	
Turker Nation works for	
Researchers speculate turkers make as little as two dollars an hour.	
Ira Spiro is suing CrowdFlower, a competitor of Mechanical Turk.	
Hall of Fame or Shame	
A smart turker pays attention to self-worth and value of skills to make money.	• *M-Turk offers options to make stable money.*

After You Listen

E. Review your notes and answer these questions. Then, discuss your answers with a partner.

1. What is an example of a kind of job a turker does?

   ____

   ____

2. What are the benefits of working as a turker?

   ____

   ____

3. What are the disadvantages of working as a turker?

   ____

   ____

4. Why is Ira Spiro launching a class action suit against CrowdFlower?

   ____

   ____

5. What is an ethical reason for avoiding a job?

____

____

6. Why do companies break up complex tasks into smaller tasks?

____

____

7. What is the Hall of Fame or Shame?

____

____

8. Why might turking be suitable for the short term but not as a career?

____

____

F. Read these sentences and choose the best summary for Listening 3.

- ☐ Crowdsourcing is a way for a company to build up a workforce of dedicated contractors who can help the company address long-term needs in online industries.
- ☐ Turking is a popular way to earn money in the short term but is legally questionable because of low payments and a lack of benefits for workers.
- ☐ Anyone can make money online by taking on jobs working for Facebook, Twitter, LinkedIn, and other companies that need help with a variety of micro-tasks.

MyBookshelf > My eLab > Exercises > Chapter 2 > Crowdworkers

Academic Survival Skill

Giving a Compare and Contrast Presentation

We often examine two or more things to compare (find similarities) and contrast (find differences). Planning a compare and contrast presentation sometimes begins with a Venn diagram of overlapping circles. The following example compares and contrasts deep-sea divers with astronauts.

A. Add one more item to each part of the Venn diagram.

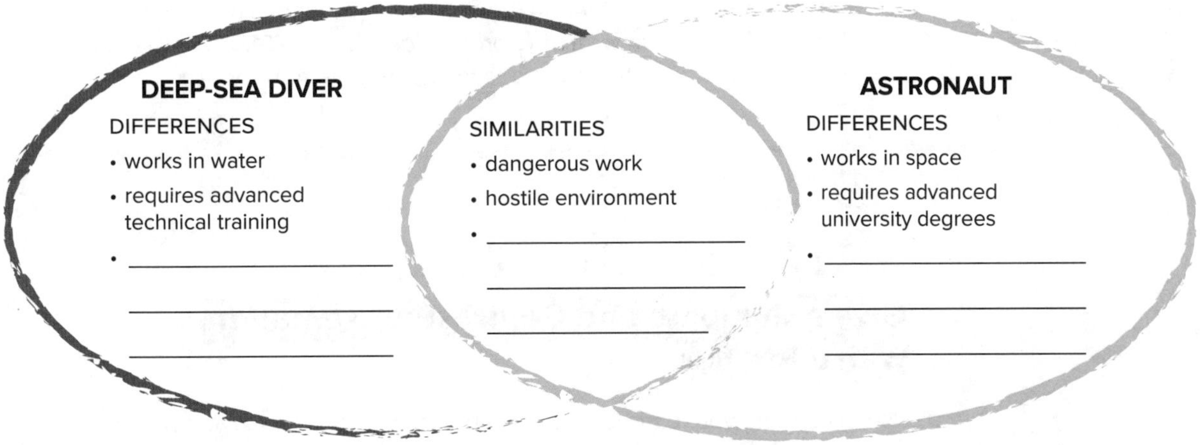

B. Here is an outline for a compare and contrast presentation structure for two speakers. You could also adapt it for one speaker. On a separate page, work with a partner to fill in the correct information in the brackets. Then, discuss what else you could add.

COMPARE AND CONTRAST PRESENTATION	SPEAKING NOTES
Introduce yourselves and your topic.	Hello. My name is [student A], and this is my partner [student B]. Today, we will be talking about two jobs: [job A] and [job B].
Describe each job. Use the feedback you received on your Warm-Up presentation to deliver a clearer message.	I [student A] will begin by talking about the first job, [A]. Now, let me [student B] continue by talking about the second job, [B].
Introduce what is similar and different. Try to include three points for each. Use compare words and phrases (*in the same way*, *similarly*, *likewise*) and contrast words and phrases (*however*, *on the other hand*, *but*, *unlike*). Use what you've learned about comparatives and superlatives to contrast the jobs.	I [student A] will talk about the similarities between [job A] and [job B]. I [student B] will now talk about the differences between [job A] and [job B].
Add a conclusion. Focus on an observation about the two jobs.	Although the two jobs seem quite different, ...
Thank your audience. Ask for questions.	Thank you for your attention. We have time for a few questions.

Citing Oral Sources and Referencing

When you give a presentation, mentioning the sources of your information (citing) helps support your argument. It also helps avoid the appearance of plagiarism—taking the ideas of others and presenting them as your own. Besides citing your sources, you need to provide references. When you use text in your presentations, such as a handout or a computer presentation slide, consider including properly formatted references to give appropriate credit.

> ! Visit My eLab Documents to review APA formats for citing and referencing original content.

C. With a partner, discuss the following three arrangements of similar information. Which one sounds the most convincing? Why?

- ☐ There's no reason to fear unknown situations. When confronted with the unknown, the most successful people figure out what it is they want.
- ☐ There's no reason to fear unknown situations. As Paul Brown wrote, "When confronted with the unknown, the most successful people figure out what is it they want."
- ☐ There's no reason to fear unknown situations. As business author and blogger Paul Brown wrote in *Forbes Magazine* in 2012, "When confronted with the unknown, the most successful people figure out what is it they want."

> ! When you quote text in a presentation, it's not necessary to include the title of the publication or the page number, but ensure they are in your references.

FINAL ASSIGNMENT

Give a Compare and Contrast Presentation with a Partner

Use everything you learned in this chapter to prepare and give a presentation that compares and contrasts your perfect job with that of a partner's.

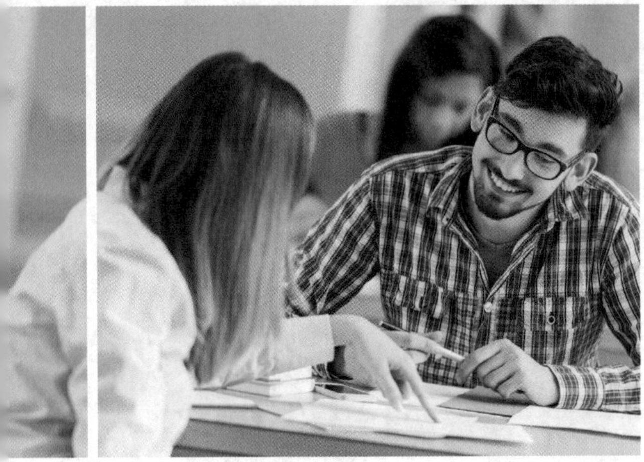

A. With a partner, discuss the perfect jobs you each presented in the Warm-Up Assignment. Find comparisons (similarities) and contrasts (differences), and organize your ideas on a Venn diagram (see Academic Survival Skill, page 41).

B. Write an outline of your presentation. Use the compare and contrast presentation structure you learned in Academic Survival Skill. When you compare or contrast your perfect jobs, use comparative and superlative adjectives (review Focus on Grammar, page 31).

C. Practise your presentation. Then, together, present it to the class. When you speak, vary your intonation and stress (see Focus on Speaking, page 36).

D. While you listen to other students' presentations, use what you learned in Focus on Listening (page 26) to identify language related to comparisons and contrasts, and use the active listening strategies you learned in Focus on Critical Thinking (page 27): ask questions and take notes so that you will be prepared to give feedback.

E. Once everyone has presented, ask for feedback from your teacher and classmates on how you could improve your presentation.

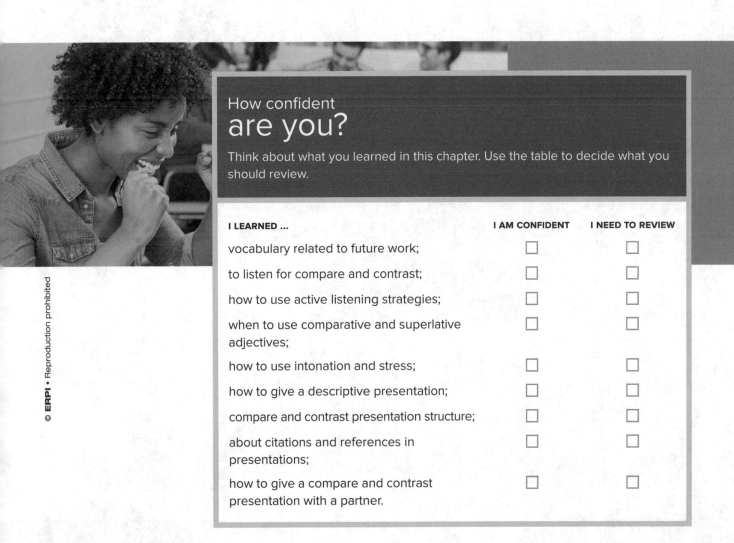

How confident are you?

Think about what you learned in this chapter. Use the table to decide what you should review.

I LEARNED ...	I AM CONFIDENT	I NEED TO REVIEW
vocabulary related to future work;	☐	☐
to listen for compare and contrast;	☐	☐
how to use active listening strategies;	☐	☐
when to use comparative and superlative adjectives;	☐	☐
how to use intonation and stress;	☐	☐
how to give a descriptive presentation;	☐	☐
compare and contrast presentation structure;	☐	☐
about citations and references in presentations;	☐	☐
how to give a compare and contrast presentation with a partner.	☐	☐

CHAPTER 3

People in Motion

The environmental cost of transportation is one of the most important issues of our time. Not only do more people need to go more places, but they are also using a wider range of ways of doing so than ever before, often increasing air and noise pollution, and wasting valuable land and other resources. Even for those who work at home, there are still shopping trips to buy food and other necessities. Shopping locally still means trucks are necessary to stock these stores. These issues raise the importance of autonomous and electric vehicles.

What transportation choices will you make in the future?

In this chapter, you will

- learn vocabulary related to future transportation;
- listen to evaluate;
- identify slang and jargon;
- review indirect and tag questions;
- learn interviewing skills;
- create survey questions;
- conduct an oral survey and present the results.

GEARING UP

A. Look at the pie chart and then answer the questions.

How Philadelphians commute to work

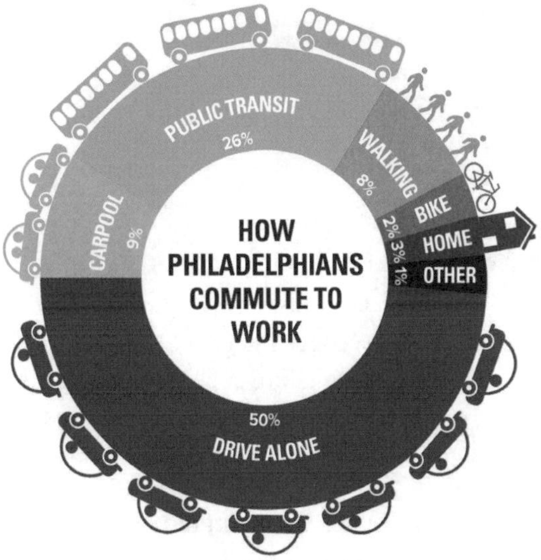

Source: How Philadelphians commute to work. (2014, March 11). Retrieved from https://phillymotu.wordpress.com/2014/03/11/tidbit-tuesday-philadelphia-commute-breakdown/

1. The pie chart shows the commuting (travelling to work) choices of people in Philadelphia. Most of them drive on their own. Why is this a concern?

   ____

   ____

2. What public transit options are common in big cities?

   ____

   ____

3. Only 8 percent of Philadelphia's population walk to work. Why do you think this number is so low?

   ____

   ____

4. What jobs are popular among people who work from home?

   ____

   ____

B. Discuss the questions and your answers, first with a partner, then in a group.

VOCABULARY BUILD OVERVIEW

Below are the key words you will practise in this chapter. Check the words you understand, then underline the words you use. Highlight the words you need to learn.

future transportation

nouns: combination, convert*, decades*, emissions, human error*, infrastructure*, intrusion, range anxiety*, sequel*, vehicles*

verbs: chronicle, concluded*, conquered, redistribute*, reinforced*, underestimated*

adjectives: attributable*, committed*, convincing*, dominant*, elitist, fundamental*, geopolitical, inevitable*, obnoxious, resistant, self-maintaining*, significant*

adverbs: potentially*, ultimately*

* Appears on the Academic Word List

FOCUS ON LISTENING

Listening to Evaluate

You listen for many different reasons. The most common ones are to listen for *detail* or for the *gist*. Listening for detail helps you identify one particular portion of information, such as the due date of an assignment. Listening for the gist is the opposite; it's about getting a general sense, or summary, of what is being said. But there are many other listening strategies.

A. Match each listening strategy to its definition.

LISTENING STRATEGIES		DEFINITIONS
1 for attitude and opinion	_____	a) to check for important vocabulary items
2 for comparisons and contrasts	_____	b) to understand something complicated
3 for key words	_____	c) to measure a speaker's true feelings and message
4 for sequence	_____	d) to consider similarities and differences
5 to clarify	_____	e) to understand the order of events

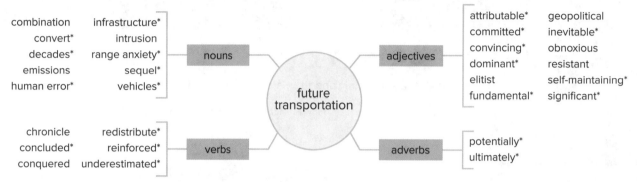

B. Among the most important reasons to listen is to *evaluate* a speaker's ideas. This means thinking of questions before, while, and after you listen. In some cases, the answers are obvious and you don't need to ask. In other cases, you may want to politely interrupt the speaker to make sure you have a chance to properly evaluate the message. Consider the following *who*, *what*, *when*, *where*, *why*, and *how* questions, and, with a partner, think of a reason for asking each one.

QUESTIONS	REASONS
WHO is the speaker?	*Find out if the speaker has special expertise on this topic or a biased point of view on it.*
WHAT is the importance of the topic?	
WHEN is the information from?	
WHERE does the information apply?	
WHY is the speaker sharing the information?	
HOW is the information presented?	

C. Read the excerpt from Listening 1 and, with a partner, ask and answer *who*, *what*, *when*, *where*, *why*, and *how* questions about it.

> I'm Ryan Chin; I'm the managing director of the City Science Initiative at the MIT Media Lab. ... Well, I think the commercial operators are very focused on manufacturability, cost, reliability, and following all the safety rules. Our research is really looking way beyond what the industry is doing. The industry is probably looking between two and five years. Our job is to look way beyond that, five, ten [years], even further, ahead. We have to look at new trends, what's going to be disruptive in terms of technology and strategy.

D. When you evaluate, it's important to take notes. Based on your questions and answers, write a one-sentence summary of your evaluation of the excerpt.

____

____

____

FOCUS ON CRITICAL THINKING

Identifying Slang and Jargon

Slang and jargon are two forms of spoken and written English that can be difficult to understand. Their purposes are quite different. Slang entertains and bonds a group with words and phrases, such as *noodle* and *grey matter* for *brain*, as well as idioms you may hear in conversations and lectures, like *sharp as a knife*, meaning intelligent. Jargon is professional language that allows speakers to be more precise, such as surgeons discussing the three main parts of the brain: *cerebrum*, *cerebellum*, and *brainstem*. You need strategies to decide when to use slang and jargon and to probe what others are saying when they use them.

A. Read sentences from Listening 1, and indicate whether each of the words or phrases in bold are slang or jargon.

SENTENCES	SLANG	JARGON
❶ The problem is actually much bigger; how to move people around in increasingly large **megacities** with congestion and pollution.	☐	☐
❷ Well, I think the commercial operators are very focused on **manufacturability**, cost, reliability, and following all the safety rules.	☐	☐
❸ Ryan and his colleagues at MIT are looking at **the big picture** of how the self-driving car will help shape our cities in the future.	☐	☐
❹ We were talking to Jim Pisz from Toyota, and he referred to autonomous vehicles as **a shiny object**, meaning that there's a lot of hype around them right now.	☐	☐
❺ Cars are constructed **to talk to each other**.	☐	☐
❻ A lot of people have a great sort of **emotional investment** in their cars.	☐	☐

B. When you are giving a formal talk, avoid slang. In other situations, if you are using slang or jargon, consider paraphrasing your words if you suspect that your audience may not understand. Add a paraphrase to each sentence adapted from Listening 2 that explains the word or phrase in bold. Note: Expressions to introduce paraphrases are in italics.

1. We're in the **tipping point** now, *by which I mean* ______________________________ ______________________________.
2. I wasn't really a car guy ever, but I was really into **cool technology**, *that is*, ______________________________.
3. Even car reviewers are **raving**; *in other words*, they're ______________________.
4. The fear of running out of **juice** is real, because charge stations are still few and far between. *And by juice*, of course, *I mean* ______________________.
5. Unless, you know, we simply run out of gas for either **geopolitical** or economic reasons. *Sorry, by* geopolitical, *I mean* ______________________ ______________________________.
6. Once people buy this brand, they become like **holy warriors** about it, *which is to say*, ______________________________.

C. When you hear someone using slang or jargon that interferes with your comprehension, you have several options. With a partner, consider each of the following, and think of a context when you might use each one.

1. Make a note and look up the term later.

   during a speech by an important politician you won't see again

2. Ask after the speaker has finished talking.

   ____

   ____

3. Interrupt politely to ask for a definition.

____

____

4. Restate the word or expression with a questioning look.

____

5. Interrupt politely and explain that the speaker's language is making it difficult to understand.

____

____

6. Ask the speaker to explain in plain language.

____

____

LISTENING 1 Autonomous Cars and the Future of Cities

The most dangerous thing you face on the road is not other cars but other drivers. Cars don't make mistakes, drivers do—and frequently. Each year, about four million crashes in North America are caused by preoccupied drivers who are tired or distracted by something happening inside or outside the car. Increasingly, mistakes are made by drivers who are focused on their mobile phones, sending or receiving texts and phone calls. Listening 1 introduces autonomous cars—cars that make all the driving decisions on their own—that would eliminate many of these problems.

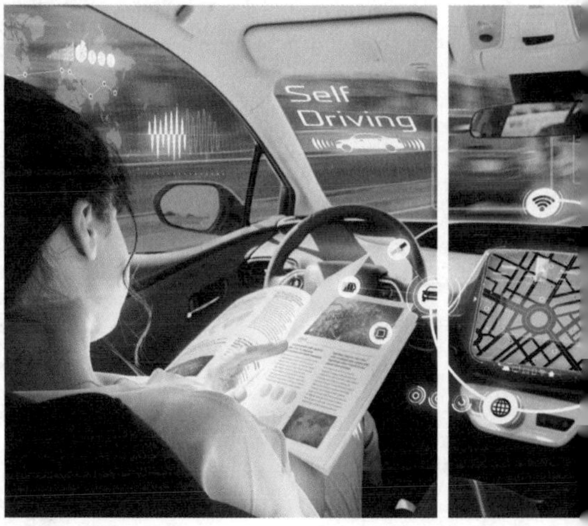

VOCABULARY BUILD

In the following exercises, explore key words from Listening 1.

A. Choose the phrase that best completes each sentence. Key words are in bold.

1. All of the transportation problems were **attributable** to ________.
   a) improvements to the highways
   b) breakdowns of the buses
   c) more funds being available

2. The city's **dominant** means of transportation is still ________.
   a) finding ways to work at home
   b) journeys in individual cars
   c) the minor travel options

3. Her mention of **human error** in accidents referred to ______.
   a) barriers such as unsafe sidewalks
   b) physical shortcomings among cyclists
   c) mistakes made by distracted drivers
4. After considering many options, the city **ultimately** ______.
   a) decided to promote carpooling
   b) started to consider discussions
   c) thought about a preliminary report
5. The report uses the term **vehicles** to include ______.
   a) pedestrians, bicycles, and cars
   b) cars, cyclists, and trucks
   c) cars, buses, and trucks

B. Match each word to its definition.

WORDS		DEFINITIONS
1 inevitable	______	a) basic physical or organizational structure
2 infrastructure	______	b) important
3 potentially	______	c) spread something again
4 redistribute	______	d) certain to happen
5 significant	______	e) having the capacity to develop

Before You Listen

A. In a group, discuss reasons why autonomous cars would be a good idea, as well as the problems that could occur with a car that drives itself.

B. Examples of jargon in Listening 1 include *lidar detector*, a laser detector used to sense other people and vehicles on the road. It uses *algorithms* (mathematical formulae) to estimate distances and speeds and make corrections to the autonomous vehicle's driving. Below are other examples of slang and jargon to help you understand this listening. Match each word to its definition.

WORDS		DEFINITIONS
1 congestion	______	a) promotional excitement
2 droves	______	b) functioning poorly
3 hype	______	c) many of something, such as people
4 impaired	______	d) crowding

WORDS		DEFINITIONS
5 platoon	________	e) people who live in cities
6 urbanites	________	f) group of people working together

While You Listen

C. The first time you listen, listen for the gist. Listen a second time, and use what you learned in Focus on Listening (page 46) to evaluate the speaker and write the arguments for and against autonomous cars. Listen a third time to check your notes.

ARGUMENTS FOR	ARGUMENTS AGAINST
• *Autonomous cars could reduce car accidents.*	• *Pollution and congestion are still an issue unless cars go all electric and are shared.*

After You Listen

D. Choose the phrase that best completes each sentence.

1. The City Science Initiative is a network of research groups that looks at ________.
   a) technology in city infrastructures
   b) ways to improve science education

2. Chin and his colleagues at MIT are looking at the big picture of ________.
   a) the screens used to navigate cars
   b) how self-driving cars will help shape cities

3. Autonomous vehicles will get better because of ________.
   a) smart cities with access to sensors and cameras
   b) more efficient batteries and computers

4. The main cost of the vehicles is the lidar detector, which is a set of lasers ________.
   a) used to avoid detection by police
   b) that make an image of the surroundings

5 Jim Pisz from Toyota referred to autonomous vehicles as a shiny object ________.

a) because the practical benefits are not clear

b) referring to safety paint designs

6 About two-thirds of all accidents are caused by human error such as ________.

a) poor road design

b) drinking, texting, telephoning, eating, sleeping

7 The biggest problem with car sharing is ________.

a) drop-offs where there is no demand

b) a lack of interested passengers

8 Private cars are not going to go away, but ________.

a) they are likely to become smaller

b) there will be a shift away from private ownership

Develop Your Vocabulary: Download and label photographs to help you remember details related to things like autonomous cars.

MyBookshelf > My eLab > Exercises > Chapter 3 > Autonomous Cars

E. The narrator of Listening 1, Nora Young, says she is skeptical (doubtful) about the idea of autonomous cars. What does she see as the bigger problem? Do you agree? Discuss with a partner.

> Now, I have to admit, I've been a bit of an autonomous car skeptic. Not so much about the technical capability; it just seems like it's directing a lot of resources at improving the individual car, when the problem is actually much bigger: how to move people around in increasingly large megacities with congestion and pollution.

F. Based on your answers to task C, would you recommend that cities encourage the use of autonomous cars? Why or why not? Discuss in a group.

FOCUS ON GRAMMAR

Indirect and Tag Questions

In Listening 1, Ryan Chin is asked, "Can we talk a bit about what potential autonomous cars have for changing the way we think about how we design and use our cities?" This is an example of an *indirect question*.

Here is the same question, but asked in two different ways.

DIRECT QUESTION: What potential do autonomous cars have for changing the way we think about how we design and use our cities?

TAG QUESTION: We can talk a bit about what potential autonomous cars have for changing the way we think about how we design and use our cities, can't we?

Indirect questions are commonly used in formal and academic English and are considered more polite than direct questions. They are also used with people you don't know.

Use what you learn about indirect and tag questions when you prepare assignments.

INDIRECT QUESTION PHRASE	SUBJECT	MODAL + MAIN VERB	ADDITIONAL INFORMATION
Can you tell me if/whether	you	could lend	me your car?
Do you know if/whether	the pool	might open	at noon?

Sometimes, instead of a question, a polite statement implies the question.

I was wondering if/whether	I	may begin	my test.

Tag questions are most often used to confirm information. Add the *tag* to the end of the statement: a positive tag for a negative statement, and a negative tag for a positive statement.

STATEMENT	QUESTION TAG
You're taking the plane,	aren't you?
He isn't taking the train,	is he?
You can lend me your car,	can't you?
She can't lend me her car,	can she?
You ride a bike,	don't you?
We never went on a train,	did we?

MyBookshelf > My eLab > Exercises > Chapter 3 > Grammar Review

A. Complete the table. Fill in the blanks with the correct form of the question. Then, practise asking and answering the questions with a partner.

DIRECT QUESTION	INDIRECT QUESTION OR POLITE STATEMENT	TAG QUESTION
❶ Will you buy an electric car next year?	*I was wondering if you might buy an electric car next year.*	*You're buying an electric car next year, aren't you?*
❷ ______	______	We're going to see plug-ins on every corner, aren't we?
❸ Is this car just a rich person's plaything?	______	______
❹ ______	Could you tell me if you consider buses comfortable?	______

DIRECT QUESTION	INDIRECT QUESTION OR POLITE STATEMENT	TAG QUESTION
❺ ________________________ ________________________ ________________________ ________________________	________________________ ________________________ ________________________ ________________________	You can't tell me the practical benefits of bicycles, can you?
❻ Can we talk about autonomous cars?	________________________ ________________________ ________________________ ________________________	________________________ ________________________ ________________________ ________________________

LISTENING 2 VIDEO

Plugging In: The Future of Electric Cars

Electric cars are not new. The first ones were invented in the early 1800s, and in the early 1900s they competed with gasoline-powered cars. But because of limited battery life, electric cars were mostly suited to short trips within cities. As roads expanded, gasoline-powered cars were better suited to long distances. Now, better batteries, more charging stations, and better car designs are making non-polluting electric cars an alternative to gasoline-powered cars. Listening 2 is a portion of a documentary about the return of electric cars.

Early electric car

VOCABULARY BUILD

In the following exercises, explore key words from Listening 2.

A. Fill in the blanks with the words that have the closest meaning to the phrases in bold.

chronicle	convert	convincing	fundamental	sequel

1. **Making our beliefs acceptable to** (________________) her involved listing all the facts.
2. This **continuation of the story** (________________) was released two years after the first movie.
3. A **basic and well-known** (________________) law while driving is the need to stop for pedestrians.

4 When he tired of the rising cost of gasoline, he became a (____________________) to electric cars.

5 It was important to **make a record of** (____________________) the story of electric cars.

B. Choose the best definition for each word or phrase. Use a dictionary to check your answers.

1	**geopolitical**	a) about territory and government	b) about mining and government
2	**committed**	a) lost forever	b) tied to a plan
3	**range anxiety**	a) worried about going too far	b) fear of a burning stove
4	**concluded**	a) started	b) finished
5	**emissions**	a) highway	b) waste gases

C. VOCABULARY EXTENSION: The word *geopolitical* is made up of the prefix *geo-* (the Greek prefix for Earth) and *political* (government affairs). Add two more examples for each prefix.

PREFIX	MEANING	EXAMPLES
1 geo-	Earth	geography,
2 extra-	additional	extraordinary,
3 micro-	small	microscope,
4 non-	not	non-violent,
5 sub-	under	subdivision,

Before You Listen

A. Compare electric and gasoline-powered cars. List what you think are the advantages and the disadvantages of each. Discuss with a partner.

	ADVANTAGES	DISADVANTAGES
ELECTRIC CARS		
GASOLINE-POWERED CARS		

B. Read the introduction to Listening 2. What small changes are now making electric vehicles a more attractive option? Would you want to drive one? Why or why not? Discuss in a group.

> **NARRATOR:** Chris Payne will tell you appetite is growing for electric cars.
>
> **CHRIS PAYNE:** We're in the tipping point now.
>
> **NARRATOR:** He's best known as director of the biting documentary *Who Killed the Electric Car?*
>
> **CP:** I wasn't really a car guy ever, but I was really into cool technology.
>
> **NARRATOR:** Back in the '90s, he drove a General Motors EV1: the first mass-market electric car. It held the promise of an oil-free future, but GM concluded it was losing money on the EV1 and destroyed them all. Chris Payne was incensed [angry].

C. These slang and jargon words and expressions are used in Listening 2. Working with a partner, write the meaning of each one. Guess at those you don't know. Then, while you listen, check your meanings.

WORDS/EXPRESSIONS	MEANINGS
1 circuit board	*electronics that control the flow of electricity*
2 smidge	
3 internal combustion engine	
4 begging the question	*raising a question about something*
5 put your money where your mouth is	*acting according to your opinions*
6 petroleum products	

While You Listen

D. As you watch the video, write the main points in Listening 2 using the outline format (see Chapter 1, page 10).

Chris Payne	• director of ______
EV1	• few left/most ______ • Payne ______
Payne has ______ electric cars.	• the cars use ______ • don't require ______ • he wants every car ______

Elon Musk's Tesla S1	• Car of the year • 0–100 km in about ______ • benefits – a guilt-free ______ – zero ______ – storage space ______ • cost ______ – wealth = ______ ______
John O'Dell: unlike electric cars	• gas cars easy to find ______ • can be ______ everywhere • marketing must overcome the ______ ______
gasoline engines	• will remain popular ______ • unless ______
fear of change disappears	• once someone ______ • they become like holy warriors

After You Listen

E. Indicate whether these statements are true or false, according to the listening.

STATEMENTS	TRUE	FALSE
1 General Motors destroyed all its EV1 electric cars because they were unprofitable.	☐	☐
2 The Volt, Leaf, and Tesla S1 are all examples of gas-electric hybrids.	☐	☐
3 The Tesla car's benefits include more storage room and fast speeds.	☐	☐
4 The cost of a Tesla sports car is about $50,000.	☐	☐
5 Maggie Argirio feels buying an electric car avoids social responsibility.	☐	☐
6 The fact that "car reviewers were raving" means reviewers were greatly impressed.	☐	☐
7 The expression *valley of death* refers to a range limit in kilometres.	☐	☐
8 The expression *holy warrior* suggests you will promote electric cars once you own one.	☐	☐

F. Answer these questions.

1. From what you now understand from Listening 2, which factors have led to a tipping point in favour of electric cars?

____

____

____

2. What comparison is being made when one of the speakers refers to guilt-free sports cars?

____

____

____

3. How does buying a $100,000 sports car "help the technology forward"?

____

____

____

Pronunciation: In words like "listen," the "t" is not pronounced. In conversation, it might not be pronounced in phrases such as "don't buy apples."

4. The valley of death refers to a point between when the first people adopt a new technology and when that technology finally becomes popular with the general public. What allows a technology to escape the valley of death?

____

____

____

MyBookshelf > My eLab > Exercises > Chapter 3 > Plugging In

FOCUS ON SPEAKING

Learning Interviewing Skills

Interviewing is a basic and important form of academic research. When you conduct an interview, you ask prepared questions and sometimes follow up with new questions based on the interviewee's replies. Interview questions often start with *who*, *what*, *when*, *where*, *why*, and *how*. But don't ask questions to which you already know the answers. For example, if you were interviewing your city's mayor about a new transit plan, the *who* and *what* questions might be unnecessary.

A. Which questions would you ask if you wanted to know the routes and means of transportation students take from home to class? Write three questions and ask six students to respond. Write your questions and their answers on a separate page.

B. Follow-up questions develop an interviewee's answers into other questions. Ask students you interviewed follow-up questions to collect additional information.

Why do you travel by ______ and not by ______?
What difference does the weather make to the route you travel?

Closed-ended questions invite one-word answers such as *yes* or *no*. Open-ended questions require longer answers.

C. Discuss a current news story with a partner. Use these phrases to find out more information. Take turns being the interviewer and the interviewee.

- Can you think of another way/time/method to ...?
- Could you describe/explain/outline ...?
- Tell me about ...
- What do you think would happen/change/improve if ...?
- What else is important/significant about ...?
- What should someone know if ...?

MyBookshelf > My eLab > Exercises > Chapter 3 > Focus on Speaking

D. Change these closed-ended questions to open-ended questions. Use expressions you learned in task C. Practise asking and answering the open-ended questions with a partner.

CLOSED-ENDED QUESTIONS	OPEN-ENDED QUESTIONS
1 Do you go to university?	Tell me about *your education.*
2 Do you take the bus to school?	______
3 Do you use a bicycle?	What are your attitudes toward ______
4 Is the bus a good way to travel?	______

CLOSED-ENDED QUESTIONS	OPEN-ENDED QUESTIONS
❺ Do you ever take a taxi?	What has been your experience ____________
❻ Have you ever walked to school?	When is walking ____________

Academic Survival Skill

Creating Survey Questions

A survey is a convenient way to collect information from a group of people. Start by considering what information—or data—you want to have and the target group that can give it to you. For example, you might be interested in what students' transportation choices might be if a public transportation strike stopped bus and subway services.

A. Indicate which of these would be good questions to ask in a survey. Discuss with a partner. Improve the questions that are vague or unrealistic. Use what you learned about open-ended questions in Focus on Speaking (page 58).

POTENTIAL SURVEY QUESTIONS	YES	NO
❶ Could you tell me if you take the bus to school? ____________	☐	☐
❷ What kind of transportation do you take to school? ____________	☐	☐
❸ You can share a car to get to school, can't you? ____________	☐	☐
❹ How far is it between your home and school? ____________	☐	☐
❺ Can you explain what would make your trip to school better? ____________	☐	☐
❻ You work on your laptop on your way to school, don't you? ____________	☐	☐
❼ If you were in a wheelchair, how would you get to school? ____________	☐	☐
❽ Would you walk five miles to school to save money? ____________	☐	☐
❾ Are you concerned about how much you spend each day on transportation to school? ____________	☐	☐
❿ Do you prefer taking a bus or riding a bicycle to school? ____________	☐	☐

B. Some survey questions offer more than one choice. Add four more options to this question.

If price was not a concern, would you go to school by ...?

☐ bicycle ☐ individual car ☐ ______________ ☐ ______________

☐ bus ☐ taxi ☐ ______________ ☐ ______________

C. Practise asking and answering the questions in tasks A and B with a partner.

WARM-UP ASSIGNMENT

Conduct an Oral Survey

Use what you learned in Academic Survival Skill and Focus on Speaking (page 58) to write survey questions about transportation choices students would make during an emergency, such as a natural disaster (e.g., earthquake, flood, severe storm).

A. Consider the type of information, or data, on transportation choices you wish to get from other students. Write an outline with the questions you want answered.

B. Write two types of questions:

- four indirect questions (see Focus on Grammar, page 52)
- one check box question with six choices

Test your questions with a partner, and review the language to make sure it is correct, easy to understand, and free of slang and jargon.

C. Conduct your questionnaire by asking six or more students for their answers. For the indirect questions, take notes on the students' responses. Ask follow-up questions for clarification.

D. Collect and summarize your data. You will use this data in the Final Assignment presentation.

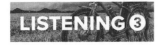

LISTENING 3

Future Electric

If you haven't heard the two-letter expression *EV* already, it's certain you will. It stands for *electric vehicle*, and while it initially referred to cars, it increasingly refers to a wide range of electric vehicles, from buses and trucks to scooters and bicycles —even skateboards. While the fuel—electricity—is not free, it seems more accessible than gasoline if you can just plug in your EV at home.

VOCABULARY BUILD

In the following exercises, explore key words from Listening 3.

A. Choose the phrase that best completes each sentence. Key words are in bold.

1. When she said that it took **decades** to create her electric engine, she meant ______.
   a) two years
   b) ten years
   c) thirty years

2. A **self-maintaining** electric car might plug itself in, ______.
   a) much like robotic vacuum cleaners do now
   b) as soon as it ran out of gas for its engine
   c) as an alternative to using cheaper energy

3. One idea that those opposed to electric cars have **reinforced** is that ______.
   a) there are unlimited charging stations
   b) charging stations are usually free
   c) there are limited charging stations

4. A major issue that electric car companies have not yet **conquered** is ______.
   a) safe roads for travelling
   b) long-lasting batteries
   c) safety regulations

5. One **intrusion** people dislike about both gas cars and electric cars is ______.
   a) their metal construction
   b) the overuse of horns
   c) their plastic construction

B. Fill in the blanks with the correct words to complete the paragraph. Use a dictionary for words you don't understand.

combination	elitist	obnoxious	resistant	underestimated

Most people buying their first cars have ______________ the amount of service they require. It's not just ______________ sports cars; every car requires a ______________ of regular check-ups and replacement parts to keep it working. Although many drivers are ______________ to the idea of an electric car, they are not just easier to maintain but they are less ______________ in terms of the noise and pollution they produce.

MyBookshelf > My eLab > Exercises > Chapter 3 > Vocabulary Review

Before You Listen

A. With a partner, read the following sentences from Listening 3 and write explanations for the words and phrases in bold. Look up those you don't know in a dictionary or online. After, use what you learned in Focus on Critical Thinking (page 47) to identify which words or phrases are slang, jargon, or regular text.

1. Their **range** was limited, and, once batteries ran down, they needed to be recharged.

   ____

2. Many wouldn't have dreamed of trying to **operate their own vehicles**.

   ____

3. This problem **came to a head** ... in 1894.

   ____

4. It had solved a major health issue of the time, reducing the spread of diseases such as **typhoid**.

   ____

5. The pollution they produced became as great a health risk as the one they had **conquered**.

   ____

6. And although **carbon fibre** was invented in 1958, it was a while before it was recognized that it was both stronger and lighter than steel or aluminum.

   ____

7. However, the major innovation that drove the development of modern electric cars came in 1980 with the **lithium ion battery**.

   ____

8. **Electric mobility** is widely seen today as a way to improve air quality and meet climate goals.

   ____

B. Read the following extract from Listening 3. If the arguments in favour of horses are so strong, why did cars ever become popular?

> Those with a stake in old technologies usually struggle against new ideas. One expert, writing in 1894, defended the use of horses as "self-feeding, self-controlling, self-maintaining, and self-reproducing, (and) they are far more economical in the energy they are able to develop from a given weight of fuel material than any other existing form of motor."

____

____

____

While You Listen

C. Many numbers are referenced in Listening 3, both for dates and quantities. As you listen, take notes to explain each one. Listen again to check the details.

1853	*first practical internal combustion engine*
before 1900	
in 1900	
100,000	
2.5 million	
1894	*The* Times *predicted that in 50 years every street in London would be buried under nine feet of manure.*
by 1912	
cars in 1900	
1903	
1907	*Bakelite invented*
1932	
1949	
1958	
1980	
2018	*Tricoire and Starace suggest electric mobility can improve air quality and meet climate goals.*
1894	

After You Listen

D. Has Listening 3 changed your point of view about electric vehicles? Would you be more or less likely to buy or use an electric vehicle? Share your point of view with a partner.

E. Review your notes and answer each of the questions.

1. Why did internal combustion-powered cars become more popular than early electric cars?

   ____

   ____

2. Why are charging times so important to electric cars?

   ____

   ____

3. Why were early cars seen as elitist?

   ____

   ____

4. Why were horses a problem that needed a solution?

   ____

   ____

5. Why was getting rid of horses a health benefit?

   ____

   ____

6. What were the principle advantages of new materials used in cars between 1903 and 1958?

   ____

   ____

7. What impact did the invention of the lithium ion battery have besides electric cars?

   ____

   ____

8. What are some alternatives to private ownership of cars?

   ____

   ____

F. Cars are not the only electric vehicles. What are the advantages and disadvantages of electric bicycles compared to electric cars? List three points for each, and then discuss in a group to brainstorm as many comparisons as possible.

ADVANTAGES: ____

____

DISADVANTAGES: ____

____

MyBookshelf > My eLab > Exercises > Chapter 3 > Future Electric

FINAL ASSIGNMENT

Prepare and Present an Oral Survey

Use what you learned in this chapter to prepare and present the results of the survey you conducted in the Warm-Up Assignment.

A. Review your data from the Warm-Up Assignment. You may want to survey additional students. Convert all figures into percentages.

B. Structure your presentation. Use this format to write notes on a separate page.

PRESENTATION STRUCTURE	NOTES
Greet the audience: introduce yourself and the reason for your survey. Explain the problem(s) or question(s) that led to the research. This raises audience interest.	Good morning/afternoon. My name is ... and today I will be talking about ... The question/problem that led to my research was ...
Identify your objectives. Describe the target group you chose, what kind of information you wanted to get, and why this target group was the best choice.	In this survey, I questioned (number) university students to determine how they would respond to (the topic). I chose this target group because ...
Explain your data collection process. Review the steps you took in preparing and conducting your survey, including how your questions matched your objectives.	My questions for the survey included ... The first question addressed the objective ....
Describe your findings. Briefly mention any data that seemed routine, expected, or inconclusive, and focus on surprising findings.	As expected, (the target group) felt ... and ..., although there were some surprising findings. First, ...
Summarize your findings and make recommendations. Summarize the main point of your findings. If appropriate, give recommendations.	In summary, the data suggests ... Based on what I have learned from the results of my survey, ... should consider ...

C. Practise your presentation on your own, and then with a partner. Avoid reading from your notes. If you need notes, write key facts and figures on a single small card.

D. Give your presentation.

E. While other students present their reports, use what you learned in Focus on Listening (page 46) to evaluate them as speakers and the content they present. If the students use slang or jargon, use what you learned in Focus on Critical Thinking (page 47) to ask questions after the presentations to ensure you understand. Use tag questions that you learned in Focus on Grammar (page 52). Be prepared to answer questions on your presentation.

F. After, ask your teacher and other students for feedback to help you improve your presentation style.

! Visit My eLab Documents for more help with giving presentations.

How confident
are you?

Think about what you learned in this chapter. Use the table to decide what you should review.

I LEARNED ...	I AM CONFIDENT	I NEED TO REVIEW
vocabulary related to future transportation;	☐	☐
to listen to evaluate;	☐	☐
to identify slang and jargon;	☐	☐
how to ask indirect and tag questions;	☐	☐
interviewing skills;	☐	☐
how to create survey questions;	☐	☐
how to conduct an oral survey and present the results.	☐	☐

CHAPTER 4

The Business of Space

Astronomy is the most ancient of sciences, inspired by curious lights in the night skies. The motions of the sun, moon, planets, and comets encouraged the development of higher mathematics. Humanity's place in the universe inspired philosophy. The twentieth century saw the creation of rockets able to explore the moon with people, and to explore Mars and beyond with machines. Each step closer to humans living on another planet produces new technologies like GPS that are useful to us all. Now, scientific research may increasingly be paid for by so-called space tourists, taking trips to the moon and beyond.

What would make you want to leave the Earth?

In this chapter, you will

- learn vocabulary related to exploring space;
- listen to infer meaning from context;
- ask critical thinking questions;
- learn how to talk about cause and effect;
- learn ways to keep a listener's attention;
- review the simple past and present perfect tenses;
- introduce an example of cause and effect and give an academic presentation.

GEARING UP

A. Look at the infographic and then answer the questions.

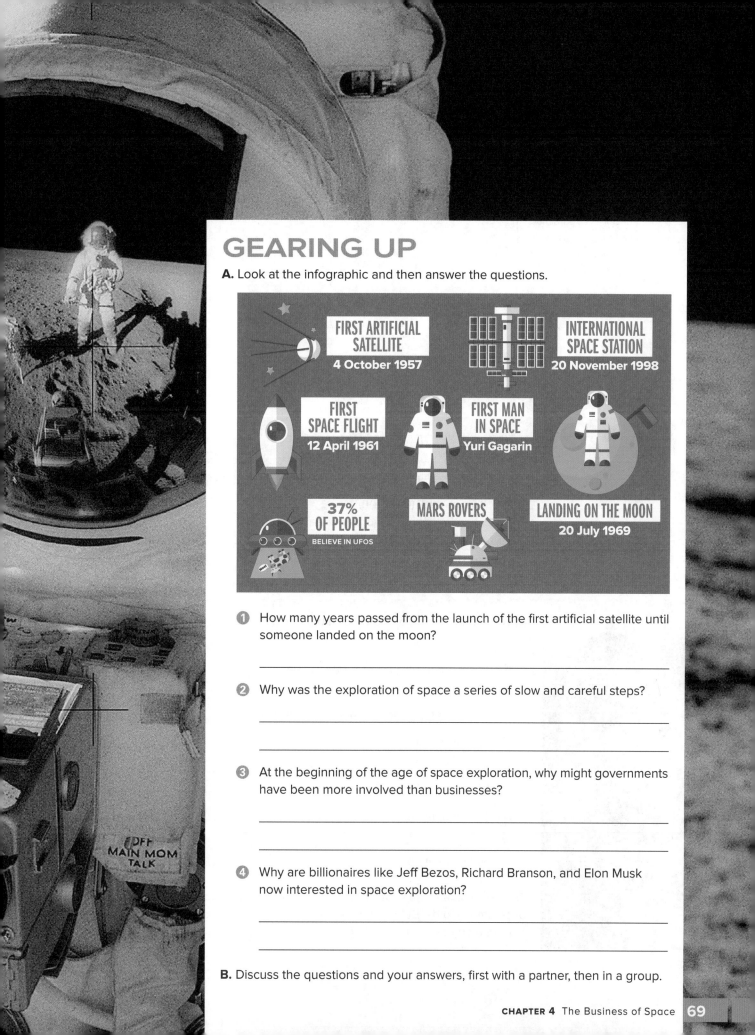

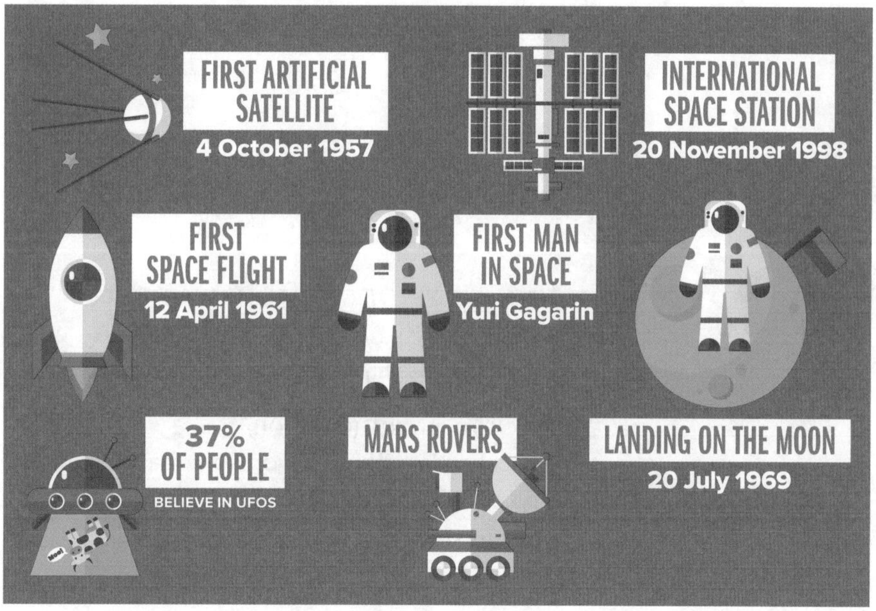

1. How many years passed from the launch of the first artificial satellite until someone landed on the moon?

   ____

2. Why was the exploration of space a series of slow and careful steps?

   ____

   ____

3. At the beginning of the age of space exploration, why might governments have been more involved than businesses?

   ____

   ____

4. Why are billionaires like Jeff Bezos, Richard Branson, and Elon Musk now interested in space exploration?

   ____

   ____

B. Discuss the questions and your answers, first with a partner, then in a group.

VOCABULARY BUILD OVERVIEW

Below are the key words you will practise in this chapter. Check the words you understand, then underline the words you use. Highlight the words you need to learn.

exploring space

nouns: asteroids, colonization, commentator*, components*, conceit, destination, destruction, mission*, molecule, orbit, parachute, sanctity, scheme*

verbs: captivated, condensed, monetize, referenced, sustain*

adjectives: consistent*, enormous*, enthusiastic, flummoxed, idealistic, ludicrous, ridiculed, unoccupied*, unparalleled*

adverbs: considerably*, essentially, monumentally

* Appears on the Academic Word List

FOCUS ON LISTENING

Inferring Meaning from Context

The meaning of a word or phrase depends on the context. For example, consider the meaning of the word *right* in these sentences:

It's on your **right**. (direction)
Education is a **right**. (a moral or legal privilege)
The answer is **right**. (correct)
We can stop **right** here. (exactly)

Some words can have opposite meanings, depending on the context.

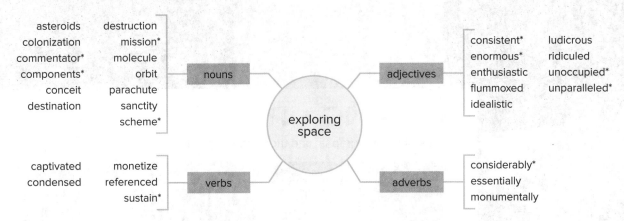

A. Write the meaning of the word in bold in each sentence.

	MEANING
1 I'm going to **bill** (v.) her for the damage to my car.	______________
2 I paid a **bill** (n.) for the damage to her car.	______________
3 He will **hold** (v.) your package.	______________
4 The cargo was stored in the **hold** (n.) of the ship.	______________
5 She bought a single **rose** (n.) at the market.	______________
6 She **rose** (v.) from her seat to speak at the meeting.	______________

The above examples show that it is important to understand the many meanings of common words. But if you hear an unusual word, you can use one of the following context strategies to guess its meaning.

CONTEXT STRATEGIES	EXAMPLE
CONTRAST: Listen for words that indicate a contrast (*but*, *unlike*) between one word or phrase and others in the sentence that you might understand.	**Space exploration**, unlike routine satellite maintenance, is discovering new things.
DEFINITION: Listen for words or phrases that signal a definition (*X is*, *like*, *a Y*) that are included in the sentence.	**Space exploration** is the attempt to better understand all that lies beyond Earth.
EXAMPLE: Listen for words or phrases that refer to an example (*such as*, *for example*).	**Space exploration**, such as sending probes to Mars, is research-based.
GRAMMAR: Try to determine the part of speech (noun, verb, adjective, adverb). This will help you understand the word's relationship to other words.	As a noun phrase, **space exploration** has a general sense of exploring.
LOGIC: Use what you understand about the rest of the sentence to infer the meaning of the key word.	To engage in **space exploration**, all you need is a telescope and a curious mind.
ROOT WORD AND/OR COMPOUND WORD: Listen for parts of the word that are similar to other words that you know.	The word ***exploration*** is a noun form of the verb *explore*, meaning to look for something.

B. Write the meaning of each word in bold. Then, write the strategy you used to help you understand the word. Check the meanings in the dictionary.

	MEANINGS	STRATEGIES
1 The former millionaire maintained his **dignity** despite losing all his money.		
2 Georgia showed an **aptitude** for running, and the other girls couldn't keep up.		
3 Your **spouse**—by which I mean your husband or wife—must also attend the meeting.		
4 He was **intimidated** by the amount of work, feeling it was too much for him to do.		
5 There are six **neurologists** studying her brain activity.		
6 With no **ego**, you would not care about yourself or what others thought about you.		

FOCUS ON CRITICAL THINKING

Asking Critical Thinking Questions

Asking questions is at the heart of thinking critically; rather than accept something as true just because you read or heard it, you challenge its truth by asking yourself or others questions. In situations where you are listening, asking questions can help get more information so you can better analyze a speaker's ideas and messages. Critical thinking questions include questions that clarify to better understand what has been said, questions that probe for more information, and questions that challenge a speaker.

A. Read the questions and decide if each is meant to clarify or to probe.

CONTEXT STRATEGIES	CLARIFY	PROBE
1 Are there any exceptions to what you're saying?	☐	☑
2 Did you say that ________?	☐	☐
3 How did you decide ________?	☐	☐
4 If ________ is true, then what about ________?	☐	☐
5 In this case, what do you mean by the word ________?	☐	☐
6 So it's ________, right?	☐	☐
7 What connects ________ and ________?	☐	☐
8 What if the opposite were true?	☐	☐
9 What's another way of saying ________?	☐	☐
10 When you said ________, did you mean ________?	☐	☐

B. Critical thinking also involves challenge questions, where you test either the speaker or the speaker's ideas. Read the personal biography of Andy Weir, the interviewee in Listening 1, and, with a partner, complete the challenge questions below. With a partner, try answering the questions you raise.

> Andy Weir built a career as a software engineer until the success of his first published novel, *The Martian*, allowed him to live out his dream of writing full time. He is a lifelong space nerd and a devoted hobbyist of subjects such as relativistic physics, orbital mechanics, and the history of manned spaceflight. (Weir, 2018, para. 1)
>
> **Reference**
>
> Weir, A. (2018). About Andy Weir. Retrieved from http://www.andyweirauthor.com/bios/andy-weir

1 Why is ________*his first novel*________ important?

____.

2 What information do I need to better understand ________________?

____

3 How do I know the information ________________

________________ is true?

____

4 Is there another interpretation/way of thinking about ________________?

____

____

5 How can ________________ be compared to

________________?

____

C. Consider this illustration of a moon colony and a few facts about life on the moon. Look at the sample clarification, probe, and challenge questions and think of a new one for each type. Discuss the questions in a group.

The moon is covered with fine dust that covers everything. At the moon's south pole, there may be reserves of frozen water; temperatures there are around 0° Celsius, twenty-four hours a day, 365 days a year. Sunlight there is perpetually weak. Elsewhere, temperatures go between 123° Celsius and -233° Celsius. The surface of the moon is subject to heavy doses of poisonous cosmic rays from which there is no protection.

CLARIFICATION QUESTION: What minerals make up the moon dust?

____

PROBE QUESTION: How might dust interfere with communication equipment?

____

CHALLENGE QUESTION: Wouldn't radiation make the windows impractical?

____

LISTENING 1

Science and Science Fiction with Andy Weir

Andy Weir became famous for his science fiction novel and movie, *The Martian*, about a biologist left behind by his crewmembers on Mars because he was presumed dead. The biologist's innovative thinking helps him communicate with Earth and stay alive long enough to be rescued. Science fiction often inspires both the public and scientists about what may be possible in the future.

VOCABULARY BUILD

In the following exercises, explore key words from Listening 1.

A. Choose the best word in parentheses to complete each sentence. Key words are in bold.

1. It was a **ludicrous** suggestion, and (everyone / no one) thought it was unreasonable.
2. The books helped to **sustain** me, giving me mental (abuse / support).
3. The **molecule** was made of atoms that were (bonded together / separated apart).
4. His main **conceit** was his insistence that the moon (was / was not) inhabited.
5. **Asteroids** are the small rocky bodies (orbiting / falling into) the sun.

B. Highlight the words that have the closest meaning to the words in bold.

1. After the moon, Mars is the **destination** where humans will most likely settle.
   a) hopefulness b) origin c) endpoint
2. The launch procedures were **consistent** to ensure continued success.
   a) unnecessary b) regular c) counted
3. It was a **monumentally** challenging job to put a person on the moon.
   a) hill-shaped b) unusually c) extremely
4. Other solar systems have **considerably** more planets that would support life.
   a) significantly b) unlikely c) distantly
5. The **colonization** of Mars will likely begin slowly at first.
   a) settlement b) poisoning c) government

Before You Listen

Author Andy Weir

A. Read an excerpt from another of Andy Weir's novels, *Artemis*, about an adventure in a city on the moon. The "price to low-Earth orbit" refers to the cost of getting someone from the Earth's surface beyond its atmosphere where gravity is no longer an issue. Using what you learned in Focus on Critical Thinking (page 71), write questions to clarify, probe, and challenge the excerpt.

> Well, my—the whole conceit of *Artemis* is based on, it takes place in the 2080s time frame and where the price to low-Earth orbit has been driven down, and it's been driven down far enough that middle-class people can afford to go to space. Once you have that, you have economics in space. You have a tourist destination.

CLARIFY: ____________________

PROBE: ____________________

____

CHALLENGE: ____________________

____

B. Although Weir is writing science fiction, his writing is heavily based on scientific facts. Why might he have done this rather than just write a fantasy novel about living on the moon?

____

____

C. Knowing the following phrases will help you understand Listening 1. Match each phrase to its definition.

PHRASES		DEFINITIONS
1 venting oxygen into space	______	a) the moon as a stepping stone to Mars
2 westward expansion	______	b) remain in an environment where oxygen won't escape into the vacuum of space

PHRASES		DEFINITIONS
❸ stay in pressure	________	c) creating fuel through chemical processes
❹ Deep Space Gateway	________	d) the settlement pattern across North America
❺ fuel generation	________	e) releasing extra oxygen to get rid of it

While You Listen

D. Use what you learned in Focus on Listening (page 70) to make inferences about points raised by the interviewer and Andy Weir based on the phrases in bold.

PHRASES	INFERENCES
❶ WEIR: And the main character is a woman who's a **small-time criminal** ...	*her crimes are not usually serious*
❷ WEIR: And it's less about **national space exploration**	
❸ GREEN: You know, I always say, if we don't spend time thinking about our future, we don't have a **future**.	
❹ WEIR: Yeah, everybody's got—every reality starts with a **dream**, right?	
❺ WEIR: ... Mainly, I needed to know the mineral **breakdown** of the ores that are available on the surface.	
❻ WEIR: I had no idea that the moon was being so **cooperative** ...	
❼ WEIR: ... we're [going to] need some **reactors**.	
❽ WEIR: ... And oxygen is really **handy**.	
❾ WEIR: Well, possibly, although to be fair, all of their mining and resource **collection** is to build out the city itself.	
❿ WEIR: Thanks. Yeah, it's building out **infrastructure**, right?	
⓫ WEIR: Yeah, absolutely. Well, my—the whole conceit of *Artemis* is based on, it takes place in the 2080s time frame and where the price to low-Earth orbit has been **driven down**, ...	
⓬ WEIR: I am, I am. My next **project** ...	
⓭ GREEN: And I think what we'll see over the next several years is a lot more thinking about going back to the moon and doing a **variety** of science.	
⓮ WEIR: Well, I think the moon would be fantastic for a stepping stone on the way to Mars, because, if Artemis really existed, a **manned** Mars mission would be monumentally easier ...	

After You Listen

E. Answer these questions.

1. Why is the moon more likely than Mars to host humanity's first off-Earth city?

   ____

   ____

2. Why is it necessary that the city of Artemis have an economic reason to exist?

   ____

   ____

3. Why does science fiction play an important role in scientific progress?

   ____

   ____

4. Why does Weir say that building a city on the moon is seen to be economically neutral?

   ____

   ____

5. What's Weir's argument for reusing Artemis City as a consistent setting in his novels?

   ____

   ____

F. What is the significance of each of the following terms? Discuss your answers with a partner.

1. anorthite ______________________________

   ____

2. smelt ______________________________

   ____

3. hydrogen ______________________________

   ____

4. railroad stations ______________________________

   ____

5. Tranquility Base (site of the first moon landing) ______________________________

   ____

6. gravity ______________________________

   ____

7. 2080 ______________________________

   ____

G. Space travel will always be difficult and dangerous. What would make some people willing to leave Earth to live on another planet, with no chance to return? Discuss your answers in a group.

MyBookshelf > My eLab > Exercises > Chapter 4 > Science and Science Fiction

Academic Survival Skill

Talking about Cause and Effect

In academic discussions and presentations, it's common to talk about cause and effect. A *cause* is an action of some kind that leads to another action—an *effect*. Often, causes and effects occur in chains, with each effect becoming the cause of something else. For example, aerial photography caused an interest in photos from space, contributing to an increase in satellites, which resulted in consumer applications like Google Maps.

A. Read the following words and phrases. Which indicate causes, and which indicate effects?

TRANSITION WORDS	CAUSE	EFFECT
1 because	☑	☐
2 brings about	☐	☐
3 contributes to	☐	☐
4 is due to	☐	☐
5 is responsible for	☐	☐
6 is the effect of	☐	☐
7 is the reason for	☐	☐
8 leads to	☐	☐
9 occurs as the result of	☐	☐
10 produces	☐	☐
11 results from	☐	☐
12 results in	☐	☐

B. Some causes have multiple effects. Read about the history of the global positioning system (GPS). Write a paragraph that connects the ideas with phrases from task A. If necessary, change phrases and tenses to past tense.

- Sputnik 1 was launched in 1957.
- Scientists noticed that the radio signal faded in and faded out as the Sputnik 1 satellite flew overhead.
- In 1959, scientists developed a GPS system with new satellites to track submarines.

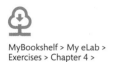

- In 1963, true GPS was invented for other military purposes.
- In 1983, the Russians shot down a Korean Airlines plane that had strayed into Russian territory.
- The US government offers GPS to all civilian aircraft, to keep them on course.

____

____

____

____

____

____

____

C. When researching a topic related to cause and effect, it's common to start with a final effect and try to understand what *cause*, or *causes*, led to it. With a partner, read each of the following *effect* statements and think of one cause that each might have resulted from. Use language from task A to explain your ideas.

1. Billionaires are creating space exploration businesses.

____

____

2. More and more people are interested in space tourism.

____

____

3. New rocket designs focus on reusing parts that are usually discarded.

____

____

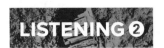

LISTENING 2 A Brief History of Space Exploration

Why go to the moon or to Mars? The money spent on doing so could, instead, be used to solve countless problems on Earth, from abolishing poverty to cleaning up the environment. Yet, the dream of space exploration endures, in part because individuals and governments want to be seen as pioneers. In other cases, there is competitiveness among governments to achieve firsts in space exploration. Along the way, side innovations like satellites for communication and GPS seem to justify the costs.

VOCABULARY BUILD

In the following exercises, explore key words from Listening 2.

A. Fill in the blanks with the correct words to complete the paragraph.

enormous	mission	orbit	ridiculed	unoccupied

Astronaut footprint on the moon

It's common to look up at the moon in its ____________________ around Earth. It's hard to believe that many now-____________________ ideas were once considered facts. For example, we know for a fact that the moon is ____________________, but ____________________ numbers of people once thought that strange creatures lived there. But, for some, facts are never enough; even a ____________________ to the moon has not stopped wild theories of aliens living under the moon's surface.

B. Choose the phrase that best completes each sentence, based on the key word in bold.

1. The **destruction** of the Earth's environment leads many to think that ________.
   a) the oceans will be the best place to live
   b) we will need to live on other planets
   c) no one should worry too much about it
2. To say that a space ship is **unparalleled** means that ________.
   a) there is no other one like it
   b) it has clean design lines
   c) it can fly horizontally
3. The speech was **condensed** into ________.
   a) a much longer version
   b) a few key points
   c) the texts it came from
4. If someone is **idealistic**, they are likely to see space travel as ________.
   a) another's idea
   b) a bad idea
   c) a good idea
5. In terms of **components**, the main parts of the rocket are ________.
   a) the engine and the fuel tanks
   b) the destination and the passenger
   c) the pilot and the crew

C. VOCABULARY EXTENSION: Use synonyms to avoid repeating the same word, but be aware that synonyms may have subtle differences in meaning. Look at these five synonyms for *condensed*, and write a brief definition for each one.

1. shortened ______________________________
2. reduced ______________________________

3. summarized ____________________
4. cut ____________________
5. edited ____________________

Before You Listen

Space pioneer
Robert Goddard

A. People have dreamed of going to the moon for centuries. What modern innovations have finally made it possible to do so? Discuss your ideas with a partner.

____

____

____

B. At the beginning of Listening 2, the speaker suggests that adaptation, competition, and collaboration have made space exploration possible. Think of an example for each one, then discuss your answers with a partner.

1. ADAPTATION: ____________________
____
2. COMPETITION: ____________________
____
3. COLLABORATION: ____________________
____

C. How much do you know about space exploration? Guess dates for each of the events. After you listen, check to see how accurate you were.

1. First person to orbit the Earth: __________
2. First satellite to orbit the Earth: __________
3. First scientific experiments with rockets by Robert Goddard: __________
4. The invention of the telescope: __________
5. Two people land on the moon: __________
6. V-2 rockets used to attack London: __________

While You Listen

D. As you listen, complete the key points of each section. Listen again, and use what you learned in Focus on Critical Thinking to think of a question about each of the points.

1. The invention of telescopes occurred in ___*1608*___.
2. Telescopes were instruments of ____________________.
3. Galileo used a telescope to discover the ____________________.
4. The development of the telescope caused
____________________.
5. Robert Goddard experimented with rockets in ____________________.

6. Nazi Germany used rockets as ______________________.

7. After World War II, the United States and the Soviet Union ________________ ____________________________________.

8. The USSR launched Sputnik 1, the first ______________________________.

9. Yuri Gagarin became the first human to orbit Earth in ____________________.

10. Neil Armstrong became the first person to walk on the moon in ___________.

11. Step 1: NASA's goals were ______________________.

12. Step 2: NASA's goal was ______________________.

13. Step 3: NASA set ______________________.

14. Step 4: make the abstract ______________________.

15. The USSR lands the first foreign object on the moon in ________________.

16. NASA's Skylab was launched in ______________________.

17. The International Space Station was launched in ______________________.

18. The focus shifted from competitiveness to cooperation because of ______________________.

19. Rising costs and benefits led to private individuals funding ________________ ______________________.

After You Listen

E. Complete the table by adding causes and effects in the blank cells.

CAUSES	EFFECTS
1 telescope invented for military use	*Galileo used it for astronomy.*
2 Robert Goddard begins experimenting with rockets.	
3	The USSR and the US develop missiles after World War II.
4 The USSR launched Sputnik 1.	
5	The US puts a person in orbit.
6 President John F. Kennedy pledges to put an American on the moon.	
7 Costs for a space station become overwhelming for one country.	
8	Private individuals like Elon Musk and Jeff Bezos become involved in space exploration.

F. Based on what you learned in Focus on Critical Thinking (page 71), write three questions about Listening 2. Share your questions with a partner and then in a group, and try to answer them.

1. ____
____

2. ____
____

3. ____
____

G. Based on the history of space exploration outlined in Listening 2, what next steps do you expect to see in terms of the exploration of Mars? Predict the dates and discuss in a group.

1. First person to visit Mars in the year ________.
2. First city of ten thousand people on Mars in the year ________.
3. People journeying to go to worlds beyond Mars ________.

MyBookshelf > My eLab > Exercises > Chapter 4 > A Brief History of Space Exploration

FOCUS ON SPEAKING

Keeping a Listener's Attention

One challenge when speaking is finding ways to keep a listener's attention. Body language and eye contact can help, but vocabulary choices and varied sentences make a bigger difference. This starts with avoiding bland words—words that are so common people ignore them. For example, the word *nice* is so overused that it has lost its meaning. Instead, use emotional words—words that stir feelings and evoke associations. For example, *agreeable*, *wonderful*, and *amusing* are synonyms for *nice*, but have more of an impact.

A. Highlight the emotional word in each pair of synonyms. Then add an emotional synonym of your own.

1	heartbreaking	bad	____________
2	gorgeous	pretty	____________
3	big	enormous	____________
4	respectable	good	____________
5	great	tremendous	____________
6	fascinating	interesting	____________
7	said	suggested	____________

Develop Your Vocabulary: Use a thesaurus to learn new synonyms, but check to see they are the same part of speech and have the same meaning.

Varying the length of your sentences adds interest by breaking up the singsong pattern found when you say several sentences with the same number of words.

B. With a partner, read aloud the two paragraphs. Which sounds better? Why? Discuss your answer with a partner.

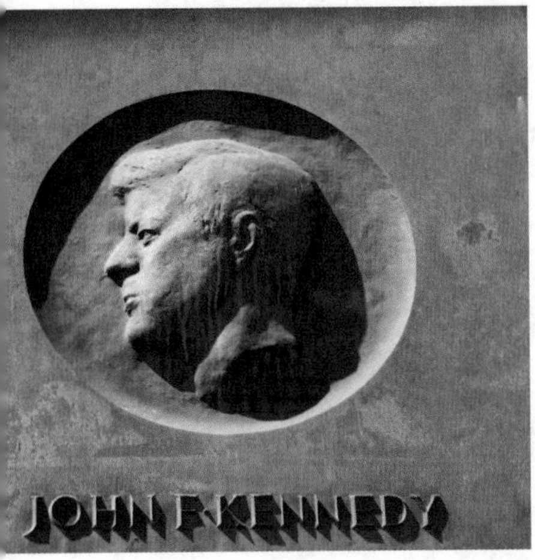

PARAGRAPH 1	PARAGRAPH 2
How did this decision happen? Behind this statement were steps. Key steps are often overlooked. I refer to work by Andrew Carton. He is a management professor. He now works at Wharton. He reviewed eighteen thousand document pages. They were from the era. He came to a conclusion. There were four key steps. Kennedy employed these four steps. His vision became a reality.	How did this happen? Behind this statement were several key steps that are often overlooked. I refer here to work by Andrew Carton, a management professor at Wharton. He reviewed eighteen thousand pages of documents from the era and came to the conclusion that there were four key steps that Kennedy employed to make his vision a reality.

C. Rewrite these sentences into two or more sentences of varying length. Replace bland words with emotional ones. Practise saying the sentences with a partner.

1. Astronaut trainees are good individuals who work hard at school and enjoy a lot of physical exercise and have good problem-solving skills.

   Astronaut trainees are spectacular individuals. Not only do they work incredibly hard at school and crave physical exercise, but their problem-solving skills are outstanding.

2. Learning different skills like flying a plane and scuba diving can help make you a better astronaut trainee, even if you are afraid of such things.

   ______

3. Good problem-solving skills mean that you like a challenge, and it's also important that you can work well on a team.

   ______

4. Astronaut trainees should try roller coasters and other things that cause motion sickness because they will encounter it in their training.

   ______

MyBookshelf > My eLab > Exercises > Chapter 4 > Focus on Speaking

FOCUS ON GRAMMAR

Simple Past and Present Perfect Tenses

Both the simple past and the present perfect tenses are used to explain things that have happened. The difference between the two is that the *simple past* describes actions or events that are not connected to the present, whereas the *present perfect* describes actions that started in the past and are either still happening or are otherwise connected to the present in some way. Consider this sentence from Listening 2.

> But lacking the clear goal of getting a person on the moon's surface may have meant they lost focus and spread their research resources in too many directions.

In this sentence, something happened in the past (*may have meant*), but the time it happened is vague.

Use the simple past or the present perfect tense to describe actions or events in terms of duration, information, and time.

	SIMPLE PAST (infinitive + *-ed*)	PRESENT PERFECT (*have/has* + past participle)
DURATION	She **talked** with the future astronauts **during lunch**. (completed action)	**She has talked** with the future astronauts during lunch **today**. (started in the past, connected to the present)
INFORMATION	He **slipped** in the space capsule and hit the alarm. (action happened earlier)	He **has just slipped** in the space capsule and hit the alarm. (action just happened)
TIME	He saw the new satellites **at 3:00 p.m.** (time is specific)	He **has seen** the new satellites this **afternoon**. (time is vague)

A. Indicate whether these signal words or phrases are used with the simple past or with the present perfect.

SIGNAL WORDS/PHRASES	SIMPLE PAST	PRESENT PERFECT
1 a few years ago	☐	☐
2 not yet	☐	☐
3 already	☐	☐
4 ever	☐	☐
5 in 2014	☐	☐
6 just	☐	☐
7 last night	☐	☐
8 the other day	☐	☐

Visit My eLab Documents to see an Irregular Verbs List, which shows simple past and past participles.

SIGNAL WORDS/PHRASES	SIMPLE PAST	PRESENT PERFECT
9 until now	☐	☐
10 up to now	☐	☐
11 yesterday	☐	☐

B. Change these sentences from the simple past to the present perfect.

1. The robot picked several kilos of moon rocks for analysis.

   ____

2. We reduced the number of hours to the moon.

   ____

3. She bumped into the International Space Station.

   ____

4. We looked at the Earth from 408 kilometres.

   ____

5. The government funded a new deep-space probe.

   ____

6. I called her via her communications device.

   ____

! *Use what you learned about the simple past and the present perfect tenses when you prepare assignments.*

MyBookshelf > My eLab > Exercises > Chapter 4 > Grammar Review

WARM-UP ASSIGNMENT

Introduce an Example of Cause and Effect

Science fiction helps predict not just what is possible, but the unintended effects that great and small changes may cause. In Academic Survival Skill, you learned language related to cause and effect. Practise that skill now by preparing an introduction that introduces yourself, identifies a topic, and outlines three effects that may result.

A. Choose one of the following topics related to space exploration, or ask your teacher to approve your choice of a new one.

- A colony is established on the moon (or Mars), but colonists' lifespans are much shorter.
- One nation chooses to take war into space—for example, shooting down other countries' satellites.
- The cost of space tourism drops to the cost of a long-distance vacation on Earth.

MY TOPIC: ______________________________

B. Outline the introduction of your presentation.

STEPS	YOUR IDEAS
❶ Greet the audience and introduce yourself. Mention any expertise you may have on the topic—for example, "I am an engineering student." Or "I've been interested in space since I was ten years old."	
❷ Introduce your topic as a cause. You can use a rhetorical question to raise audience interest—for example, "What do you think would happen if ...?"	
❸ Identify three effects from the cause you mentioned in your second step. Note: In the Final Assignment, you will add examples and explanations for these effects, so consider them carefully. After, you will add a conclusion.	EFFECT 1: EFFECT 2: EFFECT 3:

C. Write notes for your presentation. Keep listeners' attention by making good vocabulary choices and by varying the length of your sentences (see Focus on Speaking, page 82).

D. Practise your presentation so you do not need to read from your notes. Maintain eye contact and use good body language to show your enthusiasm for your topic. After practising your presentation on your own, practise in front of a partner.

E. Ask your partner and teacher for feedback to help you improve your presentation skills.

LISTENING 3
VIDEO

The First Moon Tourist

What would you do if you had $20 million to spend on yourself? For Dennis Tito, the answer in 2001 was to become the first space tourist. Tito, an engineer who once worked at NASA, founded an investment company that made him wealthy. His trip in space involved circling the world 128 times over nearly eight days, and visiting the International Space Station. Since Tito's trip, new companies have been founded to encourage space tourism as a way of funding other projects.

Elon Musk

VOCABULARY BUILD

In the following exercises, explore key words from Listening 3.

A. Draw an arrow (↓) to indicate where in each sentence the word in parentheses should be placed.

1. **(commentator)** People liked to hear his views, so, after working as a reporter, he became a on the radio.
2. **(essentially)** With several businesses, her money grew by itself.
3. **(flummoxed)** He tried not to appear confused, but he was clearly .
4. **(monetize)** To his space website, he decided to sell ads for telescopes.
5. **(referenced)** It wasn't until she space travel that I realized she'd been an astronaut.

B. Read the following words in bold in the context of sentences adapted from Listening 3. Write a definition for each one. Use a dictionary for those you do not understand.

1. We've been talking about this because it's, you know, we still continue to be **captivated** by space.

   ____

   ____

2. Rather than sending up a little capsule that comes down by **parachute**, this one is in two pieces.

   ____

   ____

3. And a nature buff. I mean, an **enthusiastic** birder.

   ____

4. You just need to be reminded of the beauty of our planet, and the **sanctity** of our planet, and why it's worth preserving.

   ____

5. Humans are small, small creatures in the overall **scheme** of things.

   ____

MyBookshelf > My eLab > Exercises > Chapter 4 > Vocabulary Review

Before You Listen

A. What are the pros and cons of space tourism? Discuss your answers with a partner.

PROS: ______________________________

____

CONS: ______________________________

____

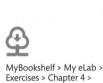

B. A Japanese billionaire, Yusaku Maezawa, is planning to collaborate with space pioneer Elon Musk to send six to eight artists on a trip around the moon to inspire them. Read the excerpt and discuss with a partner whether such a trip would be significantly better than simply looking at photos and video of the moon.

> When I was staring at his painting, I thought: What if Basquiat had gone to space and had seen the moon up close? What if Picasso had gone to the moon? Or Andy Warhol? There're so many artists with us today that I wish would create amazing works of art for humankind.

C. Listening 3 mentions several individuals. With a partner, identify each one's profession. Check after you listen to identify any you may not have known.

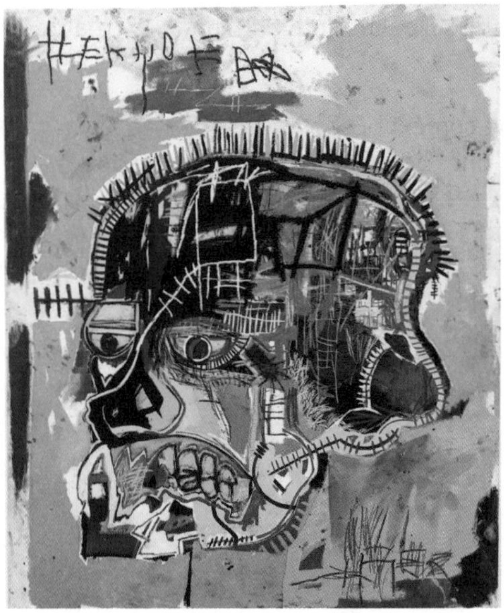

Jean-Michel Basquiat, Untitled, 1981

1. Andy Warhol ____________________
2. Jean-Michel Basquiat ____________________
3. Celine Dion ____________________
4. Chris Hadfield ____________________
5. Douglas Coupland ____________________
6. Edward Burtynsky ____________________
7. Elon Musk ____________________
8. Lady Gaga ____________________
9. Margaret Atwood ____________________
10. Paul Robert Turner ____________________
11. Pablo Picasso ____________________
12. Roberta Bondar ____________________

While You Listen

D. Read the listening prompts and fill in the missing details.

LISTENING PROMPTS	DETAILS
1 The first paying customer of the Falcon Rocket:	*Yusaku Maezawa*
2 The first private passenger for	
3 Yusaku Maezawa made his fortune as	
4 Maezawa bought a Basquiat painting for	
5 Maezawa is going to pay for the moon ferry for about six to eight	
6 SpaceX has been around since	(year)

LISTENING PROMPTS	DETAILS
7 SpaceX gets to the International Space Station in	(year)
8 SpaceX has a drone-ship landing on an ocean platform in	(year)
9 SpaceX is driving down the costs with	
10 The Big Falcon Rocket (BFR) is taking passengers to	
11 The BFR program is expected to cost about	$
12 Russian Federation's cost for a round trip to the International Space Station is	$
13 Virgin Galactic	*a Richard Branson company*
14 Blue Origin	*a Jeff Bezos company*
15 People have not been to the moon since	(year)
16 Bob McDonald, who's our science	
17 Musk could fly cargo to space cheaper than	
18 Big Falcon Rocket, rather than sending up a capsule that returns with a parachute, is in two pieces. Both parts of the rocket	

After You Listen

E. Indicate whether these statements are true or false, according to the listening.

STATEMENTS	TRUE	FALSE
1 Yusaku Maezawa is buying SpaceX for $5 billion dollars.	☐	☐
2 The price paid for a painting emphasizes the fact that Maezawa can afford to go to the moon.	☐	☐
3 The idea of taking architects is to plan future moon colonies.	☐	☐
4 SpaceX's strategies suggest that NASA was the first to reuse its rocket components.	☐	☐
5 Maezawa's flight to the moon will not completely fund the creation of the Big Falcon Rocket.	☐	☐
6 Russian Federation fees for trips to the International Space Station show how inexpensive space travel is.	☐	☐
7 Three companies are now competing to send tourists to space.	☐	☐
8 Flying cargo cheaper than NASA means Musk has found a business opportunity.	☐	☐

F. Listening 3 uses several idioms or expressions that may have unclear meanings. Write definitions for each of the following based on what you heard.

1. giant leap ______
2. deep pockets ______
3. moon ferry ______
4. one step further ______
5. digging out ______
6. cracking into ______

MyBookshelf > My eLab > Exercises > Chapter 4 > The First Moon Tourist

G. Yusaku Maezawa plans to invite six to eight artists to join him. In a group, identify six artists (visual artists, musicians, writers) he should select, and explain why. Use what you learned in Focus on Critical Thinking (page 71) to question others' suggestions, and try to agree on the best six.

FINAL ASSIGNMENT

Give an Academic Presentation

Use what you learned in this chapter to give an academic presentation on one aspect of space exploration.

A. Start with the topic and introduction you created in the Warm-Up Assignment. Based on the feedback you received from your teacher and partner, consider how you can improve on the content and make revisions.

B. Build on your introduction by including an example and an explanation for each of your three points.

EFFECT 1: ______

EXAMPLE: ______

EXPLANATION: ______

EFFECT 2: ______

EXAMPLE: ______

EXPLANATION: ______

EFFECT 3: ______

EXAMPLE: ______

EXPLANATION: ______

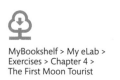

C. Add a conclusion that summarizes your points, and, if appropriate, add a call to action, such as encouraging listeners to learn more about the issues related to space exploration.

CONCLUSION: ______________________________

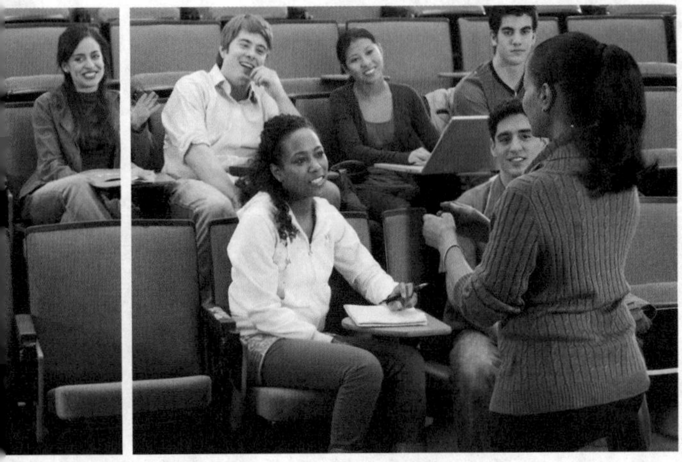

D. As you write an outline of your presentation, make good vocabulary choices and vary the length of your sentences (see Focus on Speaking, page 82). Use appropriate simple past or present perfect tenses (see Focus on Grammar, page 84) and signal words when describing causes and effects.

E. Practise your presentation with your notes and without them until you are confident. Then, practise with a partner.

F. Present to the class and be prepared to answer questions on your ideas. Ask for feedback from your teacher and classmates.

How confident are you?

Think about what you learned in this chapter. Use the table to decide what you should review.

I LEARNED ...	I AM CONFIDENT	I NEED TO REVIEW
vocabulary related to space exploration;	☐	☐
to listen to infer meaning from context;	☐	☐
to ask critical thinking questions;	☐	☐
to talk about cause and effect;	☐	☐
how to keep a listener's attention;	☐	☐
the simple past and present perfect tenses;	☐	☐
to introduce an example of cause and effect and give an academic presentation.	☐	☐

CHAPTER 5

Inventing the Future

What's the next big thing? Once in a while, a new technology completely changes the world. In their day, steam engines and electric lights had this kind of impact, as did televisions, mobile phones, and the Internet. It's sometimes hard to spot an influential technology at first because it can have a long incubation—the time it takes to go from an idea to widespread practical use. But 3D printing seems to be a technology that is likely to grow bigger as applications to many different fields are explored.

How will your future be printed?

In this chapter, you will

- learn vocabulary related to 3D printing;
- listen for point of view;
- use register and tone to communicate effectively;
- review different sentence types;
- learn to build schema;
- develop teamwork skills;
- develop product proposals and conduct a meeting to discuss them.

GEARING UP

A. Look at the image and then answer the questions.

A 3D printer makes sections of a model of the Eiffel Tower

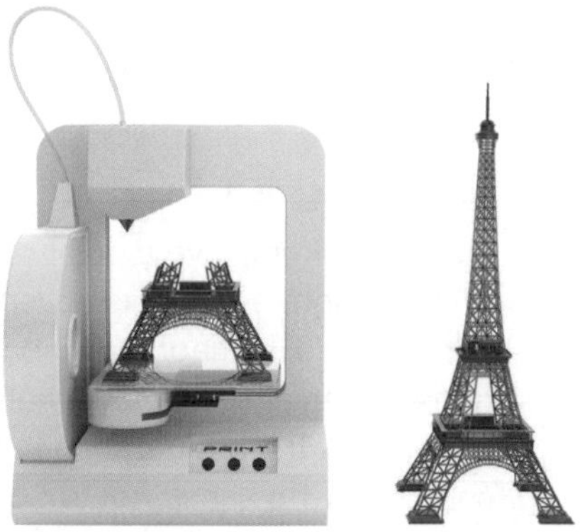

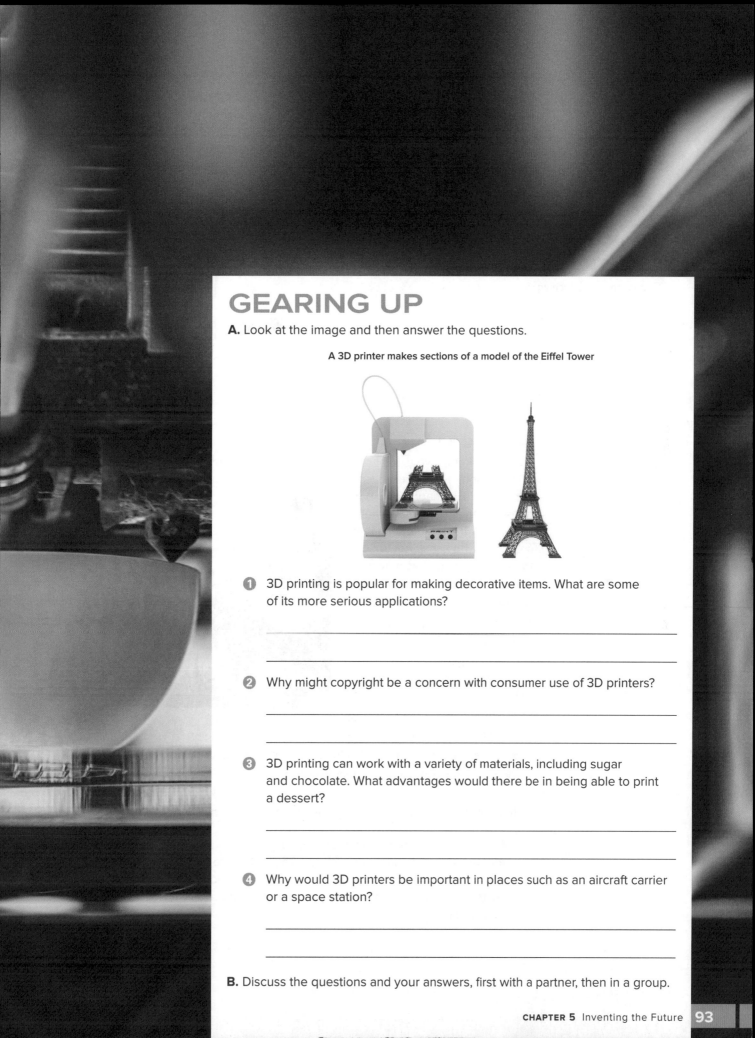

1. 3D printing is popular for making decorative items. What are some of its more serious applications?

   ____

   ____

2. Why might copyright be a concern with consumer use of 3D printers?

   ____

   ____

3. 3D printing can work with a variety of materials, including sugar and chocolate. What advantages would there be in being able to print a dessert?

   ____

   ____

4. Why would 3D printers be important in places such as an aircraft carrier or a space station?

   ____

   ____

B. Discuss the questions and your answers, first with a partner, then in a group.

VOCABULARY BUILD OVERVIEW

Below are the key words you will practise in this chapter. Check the words you understand, then underline the words you use. Highlight the words you need to learn.

3D printing

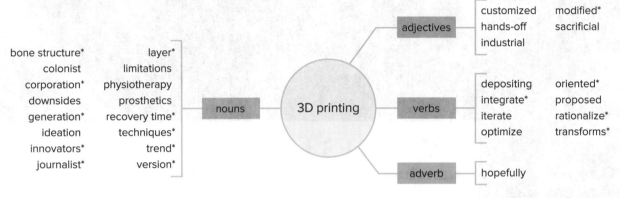

nouns
- bone structure*
- colonist
- corporation*
- downsides
- generation*
- ideation
- innovators*
- journalist*
- layer*
- limitations
- physiotherapy
- prosthetics
- recovery time*
- techniques*
- trend*
- version*

adjectives
- customized
- hands-off
- industrial
- modified*
- sacrificial

verbs
- depositing
- integrate*
- iterate
- optimize
- oriented*
- proposed
- rationalize*
- transforms*

adverb
- hopefully

* Appears on the Academic Word List

FOCUS ON LISTENING

Listening for Point of View

Many speakers have a point of view when they share ideas. These points of view might be obvious, based on their backgrounds or occupations. For example, someone who has gone to university is more likely to consider it a good option than someone who chose not to go to university. Speakers may not state their point of view, but you can predict it and interpret what they say accordingly.

Ask these questions:

- Does the speaker provide supporting evidence: facts, statistics, or references?
- Does the speaker offer evidence that might support a different point of view?
- Does the speaker's use of adjectives and adverbs favour one point of view?
- Does the speaker's language feature positive phrases over neutral ones?

A. Read this excerpt from Listening 1 and highlight the adjectives and adverbs.

> Well, we're having some technical issues. If you just take a look at the machine, you can see that it's acting up a little bit. The part where the plastic is supposed to come out of, well, that's just kind of going back and forth; it's a little stuck. But this is to be expected; this is a technology that's evolving, so this kind of comes with it.

B. Look at five positive phrases from the paragraph in task A, and match each one to the neutral or negative ways each could be expressed.

POSITIVE PHRASES		NEUTRAL/NEGATIVE PHRASES
❶ you can see	______	a) not working properly
❷ some technical issues	______	b) this is unexpected
❸ acting up	______	c) it's obvious that
❹ this is to be expected	______	d) it's not ready yet
❺ a technology that's evolving	______	e) problems

C. It's important for a person's point of view to be supported by facts. Consider three excerpts from Listening 1 that include supporting facts. Rate them from most (1) to least (3) convincing. Then, think of the opposite point of view for each one. Work with a partner to explain and compare your ideas and reasons.

______ John Tenbusch believes it (the 3D printer) will create other jobs in engineering and design. His company uses the machines, and eventually he believes everyone will.

____

____

____

______ The machines—the industrial ones—are very expensive; even the consumer ones are pretty pricey. This one was about $1300.

____

____

____

______ But files can be shared and fall into the wrong hands. Earlier this year the world's first handgun was made, using parts built by a 3D printer and based on online instructions.

____

____

____

!

In a conversation, you can ask for the person's point of view.

FOCUS ON SPEAKING

Using Register and Tone

A common expression about communicating is, "It's not what you say; it's how you say it." Register and tone refer to how you express yourself, and both are ways through which you share your ideas more effectively.

Register

There are three forms of register: formal, informal, and neutral. Choose a register based on your purpose for speaking and whom you are speaking with.

Use a *formal register* with strangers and if you need to appear more serious when speaking to authority figures, such as your professor or a boss. A formal register avoids contractions (e.g., *I've*, *couldn't*) and slang (e.g., *cool*, *awesome*) and uses longer sentences.

A formal register focuses on saying words fully and correctly, using proper grammar.

> We insist that medical professionals embrace three-dimensional printing in order to tailor implants such as articulated knees.

Use an *informal register* in casual situations, in everyday conversations, and with friends and others you know well. It's more common to use slang and informal contractions such as "gonna," "wanna," or "watcha doin'?" instead of "going to," "want to," or "what are you doing?" Grammar is less important, as long as you are properly understood. Shorter sentences are common when using an informal register.

> The coolest thing about 3D printing is your doctor will someday make you the perfect fit of an artificial knee and other goodies.

Use a *neutral register* when you explain facts, such as scientific processes. For this reason, a neutral register avoids opinions. A neutral register is similar to a formal register in avoiding contractions and slang. Jargon (professional terminology) is common in all three registers, but should only be used if you know your audience will understand it. For example, doctors can be more precise and save time with each other by using specific medical jargon rather than more commonly understood forms (e.g., *myocardial infarction* instead of *heart attack*).

> The term three-dimensional (3D) printing refers to a process that can be used to create objects such as artificial body parts, which can be tailored for each individual.

A. Indicate whether these statements are formal, informal, or neutral.

STATEMENTS	FORMAL	INFORMAL	NEUTRAL
1 We're just hanging out at the lab today.	☐	☐	☐
2 An MRI scan of a patient involves three steps.	☐	☐	☐
3 The key role of the scientist is to ask questions.	☐	☐	☐
4 3D printing is never gonna replace hand-carving.	☐	☐	☐
5 After one hour, a prototype emerges from the printer.	☐	☐	☐
6 Innovation is a principle driver in manufacturing.	☐	☐	☐

Tone

Tone refers to choosing words that express emotion (e.g., *anger*, *excitement*, *sorrow*) or degrees of professionalism (e.g., *confidence*, *intelligence*, *expertise*). Improve your tone by using words that carry greater weight when you talk.

B. Highlight the word or phrase in parentheses that best expresses the emotion or professionalism of the key words in bold. Look up words you don't know in a dictionary. Then, practise saying the sentences with a partner.

1. **concern:** We were (anxious / worried) when we couldn't find our pet snake.
2. **defiance:** They (don't want / absolutely refuse) to fund the project.
3. **fear:** I am (afraid / terrified) that he will make a mistake while skydiving.
4. **happiness:** At first, the young couple seemed (jubilant / happy) together.
5. **interest:** The scientist was (inquisitive about / curious about) the new ant species.
6. **ability:** The legal librarian is (good / accomplished) at his job.

MyBookshelf > My eLab > Exercises > Chapter 5 > Focus on Speaking

LISTENING 1

VIDEO

3D Printing

On April 3, 1973, Martin Cooper made a mobile phone call—the first ever. Ten years later, Cooper and his team introduced mobile phones to the general public. He could not have predicted the countless features inventors would add, such as cameras, music players, and social media apps. Similarly, 3D printing is an invention that many people are now developing in surprising ways. Listening 1 discusses some of the 3D printing applications, from engine bolts to artificial knees.

VOCABULARY BUILD

In the following exercises, explore key words from Listening 1.

A. Fill in the blanks with the correct word or phrase to complete the paragraph. Use a dictionary for words you don't understand.

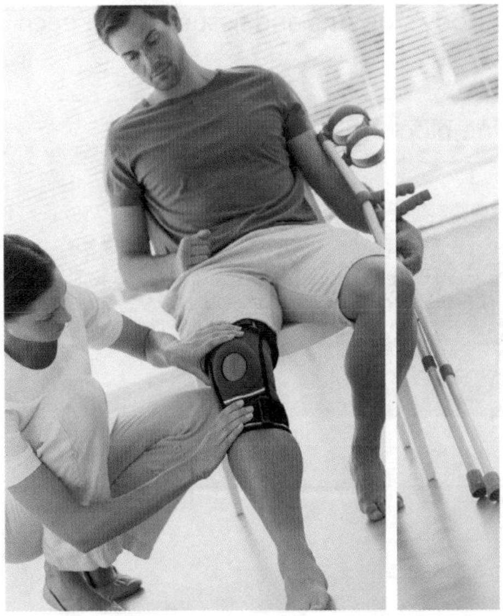

bone structure	downsides	physiotherapy
recovery time	trend	

One of the ______________________ with replacement parts for knees and other joints is that everyone has a different ______________________. Sometimes the artificial knee is too large or too small and needs to be replaced. This can lead to a longer ______________________ for a patient. During this time, long sessions of ______________________ are used to help the patient regain strength. But a new ______________________ is to create custom knees using 3D printers that reduce care after an operation.

B. Choose the word or phrase that best completes each sentence. Key words are in bold.

1. New technologies tend to be more **hands-off**, requiring (a lot of / little) supervision.
2. True **innovators** (build on / copy) what others have done.
3. By depositing plastic drops one **layer** at a time, a (negative / positive) shape is formed.
4. 3D printing involves **techniques** developed to create things (randomly / consistently).
5. An **industrial** 3D printer is more likely to be found in a (factory / home).

Before You Listen

A. A *prototype* is a preliminary model that helps designers figure out problems before constructing a finished model for mass production. Look around you and imagine how 3D printing could be used to make a prototype for common objects such as a pen, a watch, a pair of glasses, or a mobile phone. How might that prototype improve the design? Discuss in a group.

B. Read this excerpt from Listening 1. What types of jobs that people do now might 3D printing eventually replace? Discuss your answer with a partner.

> **NIGEL SOUTHWAY:** If it's a good technology, it's supposed to make the cost go down.
>
> **MAKDA GHEBRESLASSIE:** Nigel Southway is with the society of manufacturing engineers. He says 3D printing will make the manufacturing industry more efficient, but there is a price to pay.
>
> **NS:** Some of the artisan techniques of toolmaking examples may disappear, and some of the complexity of running certain kinds of processing equipment won't be necessary with this technology; it's more hands-off.

C. Knowing these words and phrases will help you understand Listening 1. For example, *magnetic resonance imaging* (MRI) uses a magnetic field and radio waves to create detailed images of your body's organs and tissues. Write each word under its image.

bolts	crutches	engine block	MRI	scars

____

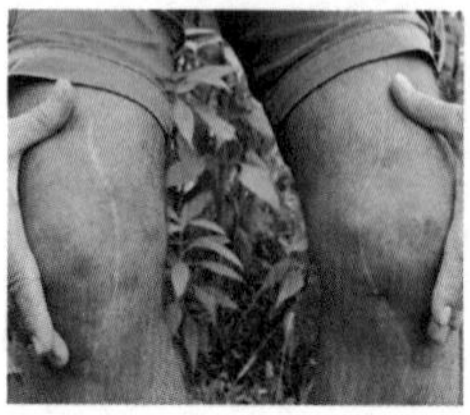
____

____

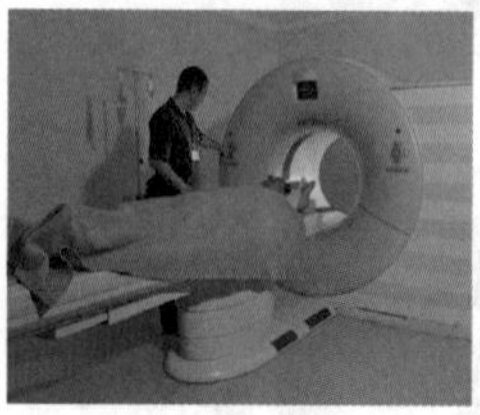
____

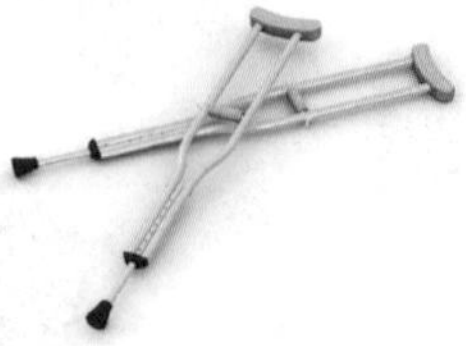
____

While You Listen

D. The first time you watch the video, write the initials of the person speaking and take notes on what each speaker is saying. Use this table to replace names with initials. Watch a second time and indicate whether each speaker uses formal, informal, or neutral registers. Watch a third time to review your notes and add details.

INITIALS	NAME	FORMAL	INFORMAL	NEUTRAL
LG	Linda Gagnier	☐	☐	☐
MG	Makda Ghebreslassie	☐	☐	☐
NS	Nigel Southway	☐	☐	☐
JT	John Tenbusch	☐	☐	☐
JU	Jill Urbanic	☐	☐	☐

SPEAKER	NOTES
MG	• *technical issues with cellphone holders*
	• *hip, knees replaced*
	• *technology changing*
	• *knee implant*
	• *prototype made using a 3D metal printer*
	• *machine lays down a layer of thin, powdered metal*

SPEAKER	NOTES
	• *use 3D printer to make food, design art*
	• *MRI of your good knee*
	• *industrial ones expensive; consumer ones, too*
	• *students designing an engine block*
	• *loss of some jobs*
	• *create customized 3D objects*
	• *files shared wrong hands*
	• *it's not the tool itself*
	• *as 3D technology evolves*

After You Listen

E. Choose the phrase that best completes each sentence.

1. CBC's Makda Ghebreslassie suggests 3D printing has ________ applications.
   a) educational, military, and entertainment
   b) aerospace, industrial, and personal
   c) aerospace, military, and medical

2. The trouble with traditional knee replacements is they ________.
   a) are likely to break down as the plastic is weak
   b) are either too large or too small for most patients
   c) can be rejected by the body and need to be replaced

3. Unlike a plastic printer that drops heated plastic, a metal printer ________.
   a) uses a laser to weld together powdered metal
   b) uses a laser to cut away a solid metal block
   c) forms a shape by dripping melted metal

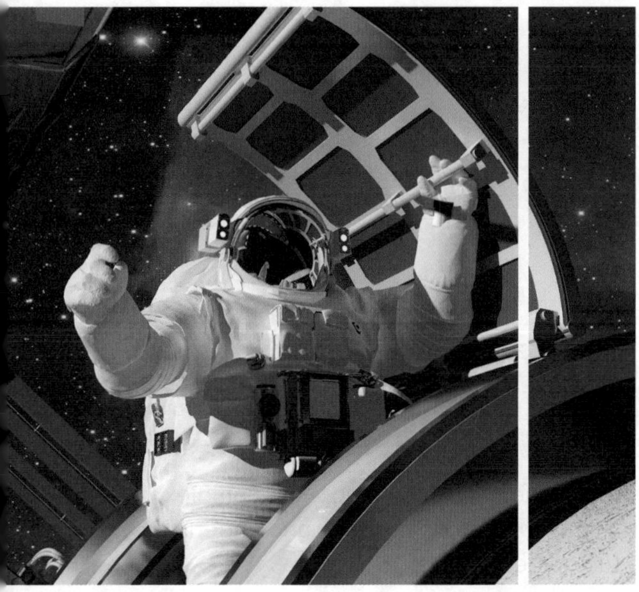

4. Astronauts are most likely to use a 3D printer ________.
   a) to create food to eat, such as pizza
   b) to create tools to do new experiments
   c) to replace parts that are damaged

5. When students create their own metal bolts, they can make them ________.
   a) for about the same price
   b) for much less money
   c) at a higher cost

6. Although it's likely some jobs will be lost because of 3D printing, ________.
   a) those who own 3D printers are less likely to need work
   b) 3D printers will be used in education to teach new skills
   c) other jobs will be created in design and engineering

7. The example of the 3D printed gun ________.
   a) shows why sales of 3D printers should be tightly controlled
   b) demonstrates that a new technology can have good and bad uses
   c) suggests that traditional guns and weapons will disappear

F. Read the following statements and choose the best summary of Listening 1.

- ☐ The future of 3D printers is most likely to be in large industrial models that can be used to work with metal and other materials.
- ☐ As a tool, the 3D printer is likely to change many fields as inventors think of new ways to use it.
- ☐ The home 3D printer is likely to disappear as commercial models become more convenient for everyone.

MyBookshelf > My eLab > Exercises > Chapter 5 > 3D Printing

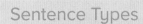

FOCUS ON GRAMMAR

Sentence Types

As you heard in Listening 1, speakers used a mixture of simple, compound, complex, and compound-complex sentences. The purpose was to give variety to what they had to say and to maintain their listeners' attention. However, when listening to speakers, it can be difficult to unravel complex and compound-complex sentences. It helps to listen for the conjunctions, those parts of speech that connect clauses.

There are two kinds of clauses: independent and dependent. An *independent clause* has a subject and a verb and expresses a complete thought. A *dependent clause* can have both a subject and a verb, but it does not express a complete thought.

SENTENCE TYPE	STRUCTURE	EXAMPLE
SIMPLE	one independent clause	3D printing is now available on campus.
COMPOUND	two independent clauses linked by a coordinate conjunction (*for*, *and*, *nor*, *but*, *or*, *yet*, *so*) or a semicolon	3D printing is now available, **but** it's not being used by many students.
COMPLEX	independent clause plus a dependent clause, linked by a subordinate conjunction (*for example*, *as*, *after*, *although*, *because*, *instead of*, *since*, *when*, *until*)	3D printing is now available **after** a $2000 contribution from the Engineering Association.
COMPOUND-COMPLEX	two (or more) independent clauses linked by a coordinate conjunction and at least one dependent clause linked by a subordinate conjunction	3D printing is now available **but** using it can be expensive **because** of the cost of materials.

Use the acronym "fanboys" to remember the coordinate conjunctions: **for**, **and**, **nor**, **but**, **or**, **yet**, **so**.

A. Imagine you are listening to someone say the following compound, complex, and compound-complex sentences. Highlight the conjunctions and underline the dependent clauses. Then, write the sentence type.

SENTENCE TYPE

1. As new technologies become more popular, they also tend to become less expensive. ____________________
2. Odd as it sounds, cooking seems complex, but it is staggeringly simple. ____________________
3. Matt Griffin says it's not as hard as it looks, and the technology has been around a lot longer than we think. ____________________
4. While layers of plastic build up, a hubcap shape appears. ____________________
5. As patents expired, it became feasible to spin off a number of cheap consumer-grade 3D printers. ____________________

B. Read the following sets of sentences and use conjunctions to combine each set into a compound or a complex sentence.

1. 3D printing technology evolved. People started to think about more than just designing cars.

   COMPLEX: ____

   ____

Pronunciation: MIT (Massachusetts Institute of Technology) is an initialism; you pronounce its letters. NASA (National Aeronautics and Space Administration) is an acronym; you pronounce it as a word.

Use what you learned about sentence types to add variety to assignments.

MyBookshelf > My eLab > Exercises > Chapter 5 > Grammar Review

2. He's a professor at MIT. He remembers why people first started thinking about it.

COMPOUND: ______________________________

____

3. I came to MIT in 1986. Manufacturing was moving overseas.

COMPLEX: ______________________________

____

4. The RepRap project started. They wanted a 3D printer that could print out parts to build another 3D printer.

COMPOUND: ______________________________

____

5. Ordinary people got their hands on ever-cheaper printers. The new technology began to change the way people made things.

COMPLEX: ______________________________

____

FOCUS ON CRITICAL THINKING

Building Schema

Schema theory is based on the idea that, when you learn something, you connect it to other things you know. A schema is a series of related ideas. For example, when you hear the word *technology*, words and pictures appear in your mind.

A. Look at the schema map (also called a mind map) on technology, and add circles with related ideas. Then, share your ideas with a partner.

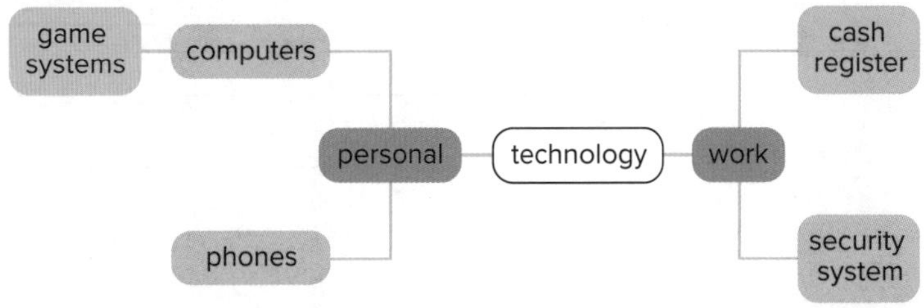

In your schema, you probably came up with different ideas than your partner. This is because you each made different connections to prior knowledge and experience.

Here are tips to improve your understanding when you listen.

- Before you listen to any presentation, think about what you know about the speaker and the topic. If you have the title of a presentation, consider how it relates to your experience.

- While you listen, think about what the ideas in the presentation mean to you: how they are important to similar ideas and how they are important in a wider context, such as in other places around the world.
- While you listen, take notes on a schema map. Everything you hear is either something you know, something you don't know, or something you thought you knew but might be wrong about. Be open to ideas that are new or different. Add these to your schema map. Think of questions, examples, and evidence that would help you build on prior knowledge.

! After taking notes on a schema, rewrite them, adding details.

B. Read this excerpt from Listening 3 and answer the questions that follow, keeping the tips above in mind. Then, compare answers in a group.

> In a June 2014 article, journalist Kwame Opam discussed the Nestlé Corporation's plans ... , and I quote Opam directly here, "to develop a device that scans people's individual levels of nutrients and designs food around their needs, not unlike the replicators found on Starfleet spaceships."

1. What do you think about when you hear or see the word *journalist*?

   ____

2. Do you know anything about the Nestlé Corporation? Can you think of any products that it produces?

   ____

   ____

3. What do you imagine when you see the word *device* in this context?

   ____

   ____

4. Have you heard of replicators and Starfleet spaceships? Whether you have or have not, what do you think of when you imagine them?

   ____

   ____

   ____

LISTENING 2 VIDEO

3D Printing: Making the Future

There are many things in life you know about, but do not completely understand. Unless you are involved in three-dimensional (3D) printing yourself, it's likely another topic that you have heard about, and even seen demonstrated, but would have trouble explaining. As Jennifer A. Lewis explains, there are basically two different methods of 3D printing—depositing layers or fusing materials—but the details are more complicated.

VOCABULARY BUILD

In the following exercises, explore key words from Listening 2.

A. Highlight the word or phrase in parentheses that best completes each sentence. Key words are in bold.

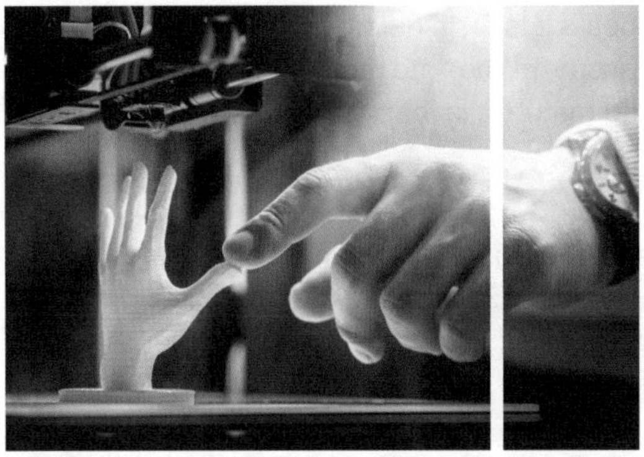

1. She wasn't afraid to **iterate**, and made (no / dozens of) versions.
2. His new **prosthetics** replaced his (car / legs).
3. This 3D printer **transforms** waste plastic so it can be (reused / thrown out).
4. In order to **optimize** the printer's accuracy, she performed (calculations / a song).
5. The **limitations** of home printers have to do with their (large / small) size.

B. Fill in the blanks with the words that have the closest meaning to the phrases in bold.

depositing	hopefully	ideation	integrate	sacrificial

1. A description of **the formation of new ideas** tried to find solutions. (____________________)
2. By **laying down** thin layers of plastic, a complex shape is formed. (____________________)
3. It's necessary to **include** the opinions of every member of the team. (____________________)
4. Parts of the machine were meant to be **discarded** in order to start the process. (____________________)
5. **With any luck**, we will be finished this project in a month. (____________________)

C. VOCABULARY EXTENSION: When you learn new words, learn related words from different word classes. Fill in the blanks in the chart.

NOUN	VERB	ADJECTIVE	ADVERB
1			*hopefully*
2		*sacrificial*	
3	*optimize*		
4	*integrate*		
5 *limitation*			

Before You Listen

A. Read an excerpt from Listening 2. What is the speaker's point of view about her topic? Discuss with a partner.

> So, let's start with the basics. What is three-dimensional printing? Essentially, what a three-dimensional printer does is it takes a digital design file like CAD—a computer-aided design file—and transforms that into three-dimensional objects. And it does that by either depositing material, layer by layer, or shining light on materials to cure them locally.

B. Listening 2 is about different processes used in 3D printing. With a partner, consider what you both already know about 3D printing and then list four questions you have about the process. Write your questions and, after listening, check to see if they have been answered.

1. ______________________
2. ______________________
3. ______________________
4. ______________________

C. This is a technical talk that includes jargon—professional terminology. Match the terms to the definitions. Look up in a dictionary those you don't know. Check your answers with a partner.

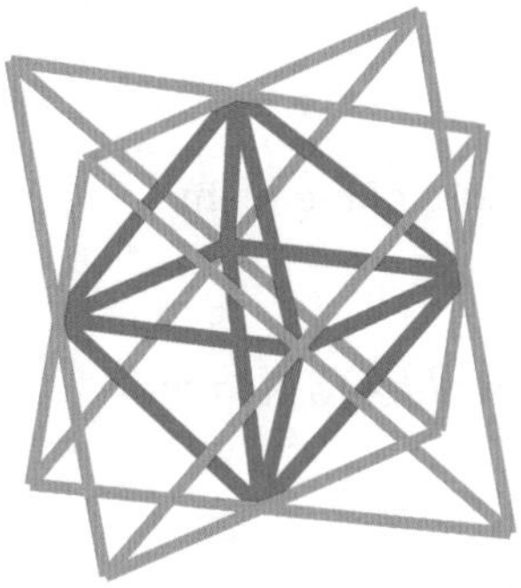

octet truss (n.)

TERMS		DEFINITIONS
1 CAD (n.)	______	a) a web on which other things are supported
2 cure (v.)	______	b) modifying something for a particular task
3 lattice-like structure (n.)	______	c) a complex formula
4 degraded (v.)	______	d) heat and make it fuse
5 customization (n.)	______	e) replacement teeth
6 orthodontics (n.)	______	f) computer-assisted design
7 algorithm (n.)	______	g) combine and form into a plastic
8 polymerize (v.)	______	h) plastic that hardens with exposure to heat
9 anneal (v.)	______	i) reduced in quality
10 thermoplastic (adj.)	______	j) to harden

While You Listen

D. In Focus on Critical Thinking (page 103), you learned about using schema to map related ideas on a topic. As you watch the video, fill in the nodes/bubbles below. You may use a separate page for your first draft. The second time you watch, fill in the details. Note: You may have to skip back to topics when something is said about them after the first time each is mentioned.

- Making the Future
  - 3D printing
    - *CAD design file* ____________________
    - Companies: ____________________
    - slice ____________________
    - give instructions ____________________
    - years old ____________________
  - 3D printer
    - ❶ ____________________
      ____
      ____
    - ❷ ____________________
      ____
      ____
  - Advantages
    - make complex ____________________
      e.g., ____________________
    - make new ____________________
      e.g., ____________________
    - mass ____________________
      e.g., ____________________
  - Hobby machine
    - cost = ____________________

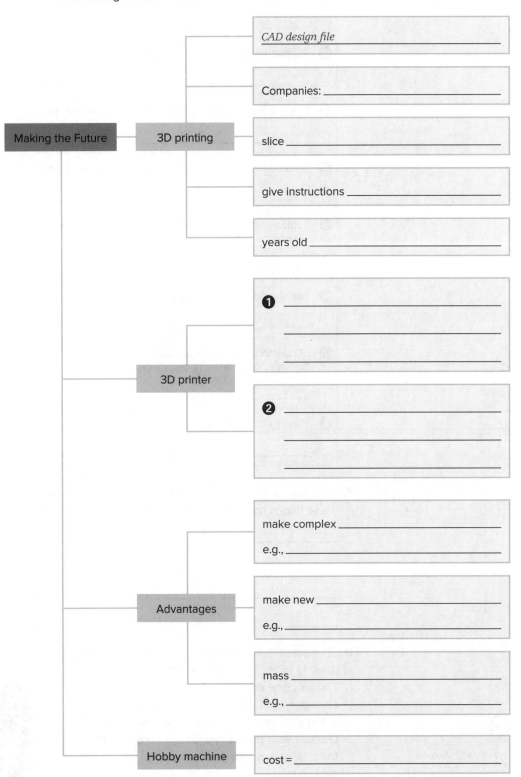

After You Listen

E. Indicate whether these statements are true or false, according to the video. Write the correct statement for those that are false.

STATEMENTS	TRUE	FALSE
❶ A CAD design file provides instructions to a printer. ______	☐	☐
❷ 3D printers have been around for fifty years. ______	☐	☐
❸ Depositing material usually involves dripping hot plastic. ______	☐	☐
❹ Stereolithography is another name for sacrificial material. ______	☐	☐
❺ Lattice-like structures can be used as a framework for 3D printed forms. ______	☐	☐
❻ Curing and photo polymerizing both harden things. ______	☐	☐
❼ 3D printers are unable to make complex shapes, such as fuel-injector nozzles, in one piece. ______	☐	☐
❽ Hobby machines can cost up to $1 million. ______	☐	☐

F. Who would likely use 3D printers for prosthetics and orthodontics? Why would these things not be made by hobbyists? Discuss your ideas with a partner.

______

______

______

______

G. 3D printers are becoming more complex—for example, printing in multiple colours and multiple materials. Think of one complex object, like a toaster, and consider what difficulties might be involved in using a 3D printer to make a version of it. Discuss your object in a group, considering the challenges involved in making each one.

MyBookshelf > My eLab > Exercises > Chapter 5 > 3D Printing: Making the Future

Academic
Survival Skill

Developing Teamwork Skills

One important skill to develop is the ability to work successfully in groups. Group participants consider themselves and others as team members. Each member may have one or more jobs to do, but together the group shares the common goal of completing a task. That task might include thinking of a new idea, solving a problem, answering a question, or making a proposal. Teamwork can help develop leadership and problem-solving skills, and encourage cooperation and conflict resolution.

A. Read these techniques for how to work successfully as a team. Then, answer the questions that follow. Discuss your answers with a partner.

Agree on the task so that everyone has a common idea of what needs to be done. If you have been given an assignment, make sure team members are clear about the details, including short-term and final deadlines. An agenda can help (see an example in the Final Assignment, page 114).

Agree on roles for each team member. For example, one might take the role of the chair/meeting leader, while another might take the role of the recorder/secretary, taking notes on what is discussed and agreed upon.

Listen actively to understand what a team member is saying. As with schema building (see Focus on Critical Thinking, page 103), compare what is being said to what you already know, and decide if the information is new and whether or not it contradicts what you previously thought.

Ask questions in a formal or a neutral register. An informal register can lead to misunderstandings. The tone of your questions and comments should be respectful. Use group meetings to learn from other team members.

Support other members when they make a good point or suggestion. Offer words of encouragement. Share ideas that support team effort.

Manage conflict by analyzing root causes. Conflicts sometimes happen because one team member doesn't understand or like the tasks, the roles, or the decisions of the team. In other cases, one team member may have had problems with another team member. Rather than ignore problems, it's best to confront them and find a solution so the work can proceed.

1. What might go wrong if some team members don't understand the assignment?

   ____

   ____

2. *Devil's advocate*, *timekeeper*, and *jargon buster* are three other roles. Write definitions for each. Then, list three other roles team members might play at a meeting.

   ____

   ____

   ____

   ____

   ____

   ____

3. What can be done if team members refuse to accept the group's ideas, perhaps preferring one of their own?

____

____

____

4. What should be done if one team member uses a lot of jargon that others in the group do not understand?

____

____

____

____

5. When team members deserve recognition, how does praising them also help the rest of the team?

____

____

____

B. In a group, read the three conflicts and discuss how you would handle each one.

CONFLICT 1:	One team member refuses to accept the group's understanding of the task and its details.
CONFLICT 2:	One team member avoids responsibilities: does not fully participate and misses deadlines.
CONFLICT 3:	One team member is unhappy with a particular role and is disruptive and delays the project.

WARM-UP ASSIGNMENT

Develop Product Proposals

In this Warm-Up Assignment, form groups of three and think about a new product suitable for 3D printing using metal, plastic, and/or wood. The product you imagine should help people living in shelters after a disaster, such as an earthquake, a flood, or a tsunami.

A. In your group, brainstorm for ideas; encourage suggestions for different options without criticizing. Use the teamwork skills you learned in Academic Survival Skill. Remember to use a variety of sentence types (see Focus on Grammar, page 101) to make your ideas more engaging.

B. Together, decide on the three best 3D printing job ideas, and have each group member choose one to present in the Final Assignment meeting (page 114).

During a natural disaster, many people will lose their eyeglasses. These could be 3D printed in plastic.

C. Prepare notes on the products to be printed. Use this format.

My choice of 3D printed product is ______________________. This product would be printed in (metal, plastic, wood). I believe it would help people living in shelters after a/an (earthquake, flood, or tsunami) because ...

D. Practise your presentation with your group. Use a formal register and respectful tone as you learned in Focus on Speaking (page 96).

E. Ask for feedback from your group members on how you could improve your presentation. As a group, reflect on how successful you were in working as a team.

LISTENING 3

Printing the Edible

Herman Potočnik (1892–1929) was an early rocket scientist who imagined a series of orbiting satellites that could be used to bounce radio signals around the world. It took thirty years for his dream to become a reality; today, it's a critical part of our ability to communicate, watch television, and use the Internet. The world needs dreamers to imagine the future as well as others who can build it. In Listening 3, learn how 3D printing was also imagined by science fiction writers, years before it became a reality.

VOCABULARY BUILD

In the following exercises, explore key words from Listening 3.

A. Choose the synonym (word with a similar meaning) for the word in bold in each sentence.

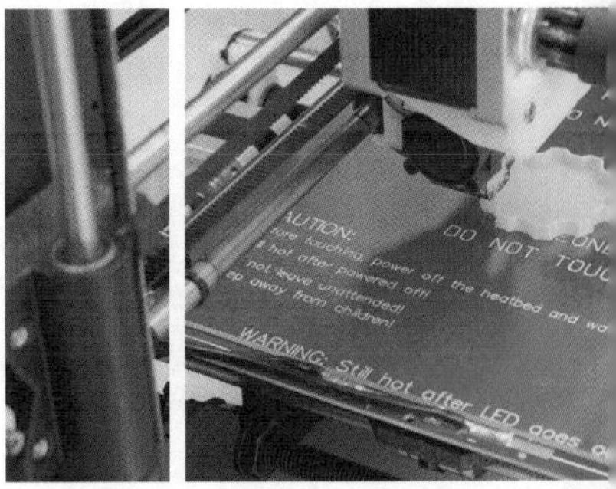

1. The ability to make **customized** parts means more repairs and fewer replacements.
   a) paid b) plastic c) tailored
2. The **corporation** had a responsibility to its shareholders to develop new products.
   a) business b) inventor c) employees
3. The **journalist** refused to give up the name of her source.
   a) editor b) reporter c) correspondent
4. We were able to **rationalize** the cost of the 3D printer because we could rent it out.
   a) justify b) diminish c) increase
5. The team **proposed** including 3D printers on ships.
   a) suggested b) refused c) questioned

B. Choose the best definition for each word. Use a dictionary to check your answers.

1. **version** a) older form of something b) particular form of something
2. **modified** a) traditionally and naturally grown b) changed from its original form
3. **generation** a) people born at the same time b) continuously recreate something

MyBookshelf > My eLab > Exercises > Chapter 5 > Vocabulary Review

4	**oriented**	a) set in the direction of something	b) set in the direction of Asia
5	**colonist**	a) a pioneer in a place or field	b) a person in charge of a prison or other group

Before You Listen

A. On a separate page, draw a schema map on 3D printing (see Focus on Critical Thinking, task A, page 103, for a model). Use the schema map to note what you already know about 3D printing as well as what you are unsure of or don't know. You can use different colours to explore these ideas. After you listen, add to your schema map.

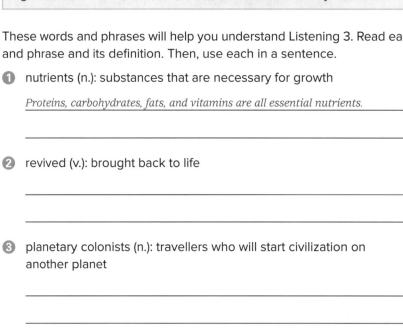

B. 3D printers have been compared to *replicators*, science fiction machines that can make almost anything, including a wide range of foods. Read this excerpt from Listening 3 and discuss in a group whether or not you would want a food replicator at home.

> Artificial meats. Labs are growing and testing them now. But similar ideas have been around for centuries. Some Chinese vegetarian restaurants offer all varieties of meat and fish made from soybeans, mushrooms, and other non-meat ingredients; the look, the taste, and the flavours are nearly identical.

C. These words and phrases will help you understand Listening 3. Read each word and phrase and its definition. Then, use each in a sentence.

1. nutrients (n.): substances that are necessary for growth

   Proteins, carbohydrates, fats, and vitamins are all essential nutrients.

2. revived (v.): brought back to life

3. planetary colonists (n.): travellers who will start civilization on another planet

4. counterpart (n.): something (or someone) with the same function

5. train of thought (n.): a series of related ideas

While You Listen

D. Use the timeline to summarize each author's idea or innovation.

DATE	SOURCE	INNOVATION
1867	Jules Verne, *From the Earth to the Moon*	
1879	Edward Page Mitchell, *The Senator's Daughter*	
1912	Edgar Rice Burroughs, *A Princess of Mars*	
1913	L. Frank Baum, *The Patchwork Girl of Oz*	
1948	Robert Heinlein, *Space Cadet*	
1966–1969	Gene Roddenberry's television series *Star Trek*	
1995	Neal Stephenson, *The Diamond Age: Or, a Young Lady's Illustrated Primer*	
2003	Margaret Atwood, *Oryx and Crake*	
2014	Kwame Opam, article	*Nestlé device scans people's nutrients and …*

After You Listen

E. Highlight the word or phrase in parentheses that best completes each sentence.

The earliest science fiction stories to talk about food mentioned (replicators / preserved foods). In one story, food was delivered by (robots / aliens). In other science fiction stories, food pills were used to provide many (tastes / meals) at once. Science fiction tended to follow scientific discoveries. For example, after microwave ovens were invented, they appeared in science fiction (one year / five years) later. Novels also tended to recognize social issues: the poor were fed by machines that used (seaweed / fish paste) as the main ingredient. But just as science fiction has sometimes followed science, the opposite is happening and a company called SMRC is developing a microwave oven-like device to feed (space travellers and colonists / sailors and polar explorers).

F. Number the following sentences in the correct order to create a summary of Listening 3.

_______ Babbage discusses the use of fish paste and genetically modified chickens.

___*1*___ Charles Preston interviews science fiction historian Sarah Babbage.

_______ Preston asks about early science fiction ideas on food in space.

_______ Babbage says she is not interested in having a machine to make her food.

_______ Preston asks Babbage about Starfleet.

_______ Babbage explains about preserved food, pills, robot waiters, and microwave ovens.

_______ Babbage explains it's a reference to a TV series and a replicator.

MyBookshelf > My eLab > Exercises > Chapter 5 > Printing the Edible

FINAL ASSIGNMENT

Conduct a Meeting to Discuss Proposals

Meet with another group and present the 3D printed product proposals that your group developed in the Warm-Up Assignment.

A. Re-form your Warm-Up Assignment groups.

B. Join a second group and plan the meeting. Use Academic Survival Skill (page 109) techniques to work successfully as a team. Make sure everyone understands the purpose of the meeting and assign key roles.

C. As a group, decide on the meeting's agenda. Ask the recorder/secretary to take notes. Use this table as a model.

AGENDA	
TITLE OF THE MEETING	Choose the best 3D printed product proposal.
PLACE	
DATE/TIME	
BUSINESS (WHAT WILL BE DISCUSSED)	Each group member will present a proposal for a 3D printed product.
ROLES	Chair: _______ Recorder/Secretary: _______ Timekeeper: _______ Other: _______
PRESENTATIONS	PROPOSAL 1: _______ PROPOSAL 2: _______ PROPOSAL 3: _______ PROPOSAL 4: _______ PROPOSAL 5: _______ PROPOSAL 6: _______
GROUP DISCUSSION	Discuss the six proposals. Ask questions to get additional information or for clarification.
VOTE	As a group, vote for the best proposal. Note: Group members cannot vote for their own proposal.

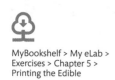

D. Follow the agenda. Have group members present their proposals. Other group members can ask questions, but the meeting leader and the timekeeper will need to pay attention to the amount of time available.

E. During the presentations and discussions, as group members, use a variety of sentence types (see Focus on Grammar, page 101) to make your ideas, comments, and suggestions more engaging. Use a formal or neutral register and a respectful tone (Focus on Speaking, page 96) to keep the meeting business-like.

F. When the presentations are finished, as a group, vote for the best proposal.

G. Reflect on your presentation and how well you contributed to the group. What could you improve?

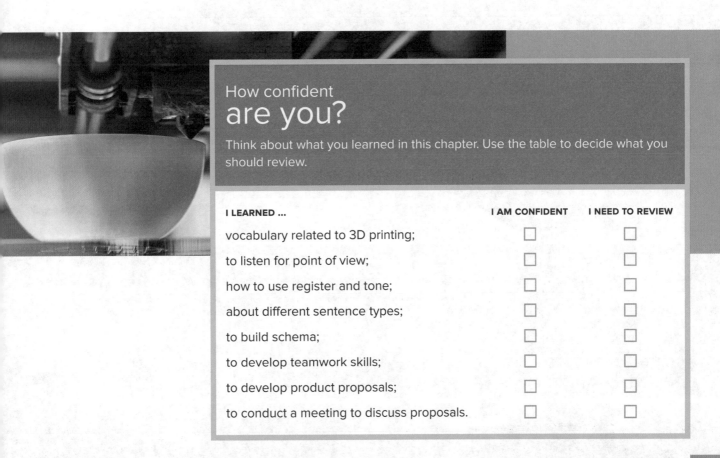

How confident are you?

Think about what you learned in this chapter. Use the table to decide what you should review.

I LEARNED ...	I AM CONFIDENT	I NEED TO REVIEW
vocabulary related to 3D printing;	☐	☐
to listen for point of view;	☐	☐
how to use register and tone;	☐	☐
about different sentence types;	☐	☐
to build schema;	☐	☐
to develop teamwork skills;	☐	☐
to develop product proposals;	☐	☐
to conduct a meeting to discuss proposals.	☐	☐

CHAPTER 6

Engineering the Future

We have always created tools to improve our abilities and help us engage in a greater variety of tasks. Books are tools that help us to remember details our brains would forget. Tools such as telescopes and microscopes have extended our vision. For the differently abled, personalized wheelchairs have allowed for a greater range of speed and motion. Some tools have given us the chance to track medical and fitness details, and others help us understand our DNA. Physical enhancements now include both new technologies that are implanted directly into the body and artificial organs.

How would you use technology to enhance your health and fitness?

In this chapter, you will

- learn vocabulary related to health and fitness;
- predict and infer ideas;
- use thought experiments to explore ideas;
- review conditional sentences;
- learn how to paraphrase and summarize;
- summarize an interview;
- use aids when speaking;
- summarize a lecture and participate in a group discussion.

GEARING UP

A. Look at the illustration and then answer the questions.

Activity tracker data

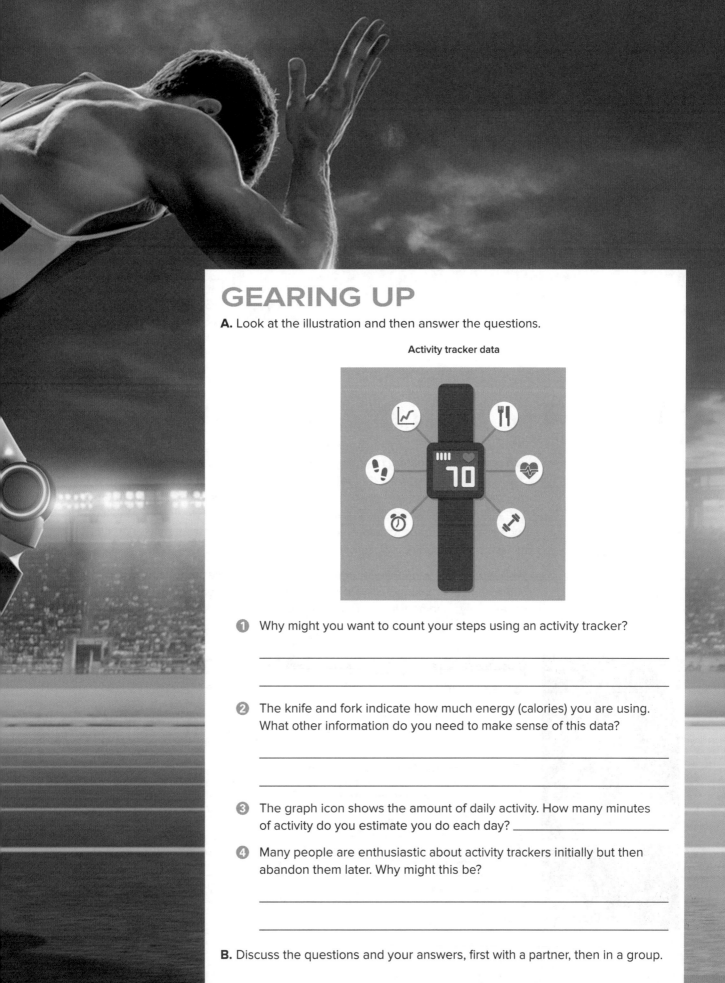

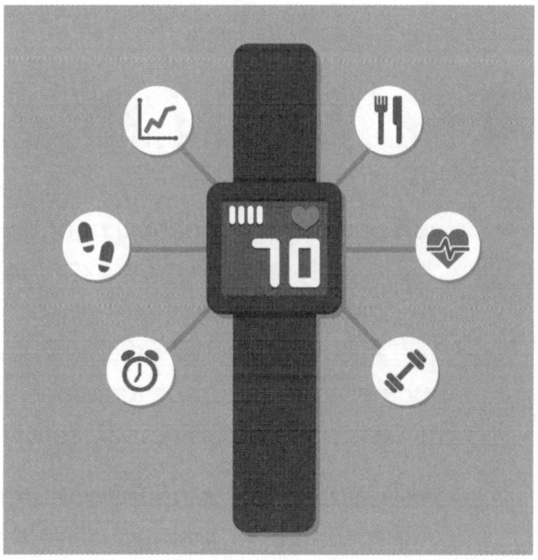

1. Why might you want to count your steps using an activity tracker?

   ____

   ____

2. The knife and fork indicate how much energy (calories) you are using. What other information do you need to make sense of this data?

   ____

   ____

3. The graph icon shows the amount of daily activity. How many minutes of activity do you estimate you do each day? ________________

4. Many people are enthusiastic about activity trackers initially but then abandon them later. Why might this be?

   ____

   ____

B. Discuss the questions and your answers, first with a partner, then in a group.

VOCABULARY BUILD OVERVIEW

Below are the key words you will practise in this chapter. Check the words you understand, then underline the words you use. Highlight the words you need to learn.

health and fitness

nouns
- access*
- achievements*
- adaptation*
- ancestors
- dimensions*
- distinction*
- enhancements*
- evolution*
- frontier
- scenario*
- spectrum

verbs
- anchors
- discriminate*
- evaluating*
- extrapolated
- registering*
- resolved*
- restrict*
- trigger*
- upgraded*

adverbs
- further*
- intensely*

adjectives
- accurate*
- cognitive
- equitable
- extinct
- overwhelming
- radical*
- sophisticated

* Appears on the Academic Word List

FOCUS ON LISTENING

Predicting and Inferring Ideas

The concepts *predicting* and *inferring* are about guessing. Before you listen, you predict what you will hear based on your knowledge of the speaker, the title of the topic, and the context of the presentation. For example, you may know the speaker's level of expertise, and you may have some ideas about the topic. The title may give you a clue about the speaker's point of view. The context, such as a classroom, a political meeting room, or a club, may help you predict as well.

While you listen, you make inferences—informed guesses that help you understand the meaning of what is said. Much of this is based on what the speaker says and how it's said. Look at the following table. Practise using the signal words and phrases in sentences with a partner.

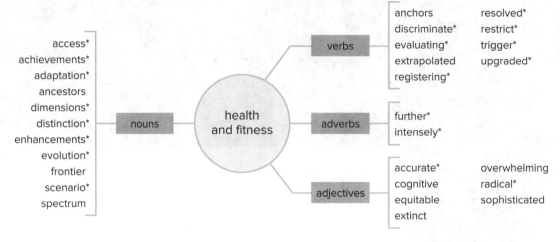

DOES THE SPEAKER	SIGNAL WORDS AND PHRASES AND OTHER INDICATORS
❶ state opinions?	I think ... / I feel ... / Some people agree ... / It's widely thought ... / I have to say ...
❷ state facts?	According to ... / A recent study says ... / It's been demonstrated that ... / Research shows ...
❸ explain the speech's purpose?	My reason for speaking today ... / I'd like to explain ... / A problem we face is [followed by a solution].
❹ stress some words or phrases more than others?	Some people *might* think ... / It was the *first* issue ... / The *most* important point ...
❺ emphasize points with gestures or expressions?	pointing / slicing the air with one's hands / nodding or shaking one's head / smiling or frowning
❻ avoid some topics?	We don't have time to talk about ... / I'm not going to explain ... / We don't have time to discuss ... [or no mention of the topic].

A. Read this excerpt from Listening 2. Mark the point where you are able to infer the topic being discussed by the words and ideas that come before it. Then, from the above table, identify what the speaker says that helps you infer meaning.

> If I can just backtrack for a moment, let me explain how I became interested in this topic. I'd have to say that I blame my father. When I was young, my father—who wore thick glasses—jokingly called me his "eagle-eyed daughter." At the time, I wondered what it would be like to have an eagle's vision, and, with a little research, I found out.

____

____

____

____

____

Predictions and inferences require information; avoid jumping to conclusions if you don't know enough.

B. Read these statements from the listenings. Discuss with a partner what you might infer from each one.

- However, for you to accomplish [an eagle's] wide vision feat would mean repositioning your eyes on the sides of your head.
- I understand that we've made a lot of progress since then.
- It's believed that Leonardo da Vinci (1452–1519) was responsible for the idea for the first pedometer, a mechanical tool that measures steps.
- The newest models [of activity trackers] have sensors to detect motion in three dimensions, using what's called a *three-access accelerometer*; that's the biggest difference from the old-generation pedometers.

FOCUS ON CRITICAL THINKING

Using Thought Experiments to Explore Ideas

What if every newborn baby was implanted with an activity tracker? It's an absurd idea, but typical of a thought experiment. A thought experiment tries to explore ideas by imagining a situation that might be impossible, particularly in terms of today's morals, laws, or technologies. The point is not to suggest that something unusual should be done but rather to examine the positive and negative consequences, leading to new ideas, such as fitness trackers for young children.

A. A famous thought experiment is about whether you would save a stranger who is drowning, even if it meant you would ruin your expensive shoes. Of course, the answer is *Yes!* But does that mean you should care just as much about strangers you might save in some way on the other side of the world? Discuss with a partner and explain your answer.

B. Consider this thought experiment, and then discuss the positive and negative consequences with a partner. Imagine if activity trackers checked your heart rate, breathing rate, exercise level, food and water intake, sleep activity and duration, and other measures, and this information was sent directly to your doctor for monitoring.

POSITIVE CONSEQUENCES: ______________________________

____

____

NEGATIVE CONSEQUENCES: ______________________________

____

____

C. When someone presents a thought experiment, it often begins with the conjunction *if*, words like *imagine*, or phrases like *should we*. Write your own thought experiment about one enhancement that might improve some people's senses to superhero levels. In a group, discuss the positive and negative consequences of such an innovation, particularly if it were only available to the wealthy.

MY THOUGHT EXPERIMENT QUESTION: ______________________________

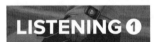

____

____

LISTENING 1

Activity Trackers and Apps

It's believed that Leonardo da Vinci (1452–1519) was responsible for the idea for the first pedometer, a mechanical tool that measures steps. The modern equivalent is the activity tracker, a device that builds on the mechanical pedometer to estimate everything from the calories you burn to your sleep patterns. By giving you feedback on your exercise routines, sleep habits, and state of well-being, activity trackers aim to motivate you to lead a healthier life. In Listening 1, longevity columnist Sharon Basaraba reviews the best features of several activity trackers.

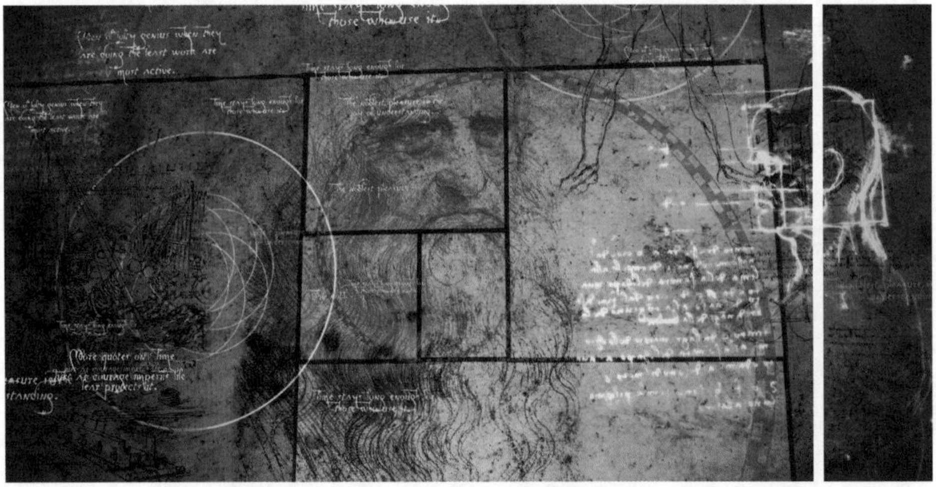

VOCABULARY BUILD

In the following exercises, explore key words from Listening 1.

A. Match each word to its definition.

WORDS		DEFINITIONS
1 achievements	______	a) extended one idea to others
2 dimensions	______	b) detecting something
3 intensely	______	c) things done successfully that make you proud
4 registering	______	d) aspects of something
5 extrapolated	______	e) with extreme force or strength

B. Choose the phrase that best completes each sentence. Key words are in bold.

1. They **resolved** the problem at the meeting, so ______.
   a) they continued to discuss it
   b) no more needed to be said
   c) it seemed impossible

2. After repeating the experiment, the results were shown to be **accurate** and ______.
   a) were accepted by everyone
   b) made the scientists try again
   c) had to be thrown out

3. There are simple enhancements like contact lenses and **sophisticated** ______.
   a) ones like implants
   b) ways to do them
   c) simpler ones

4. In terms of **access** to the building, ______.
   a) everyone could use the front door
   b) there was no way to get in
   c) people could exit underground

Before You Listen

A. Activity trackers typically measure heart rate, calories burned, and distances covered, both in steps and kilometres. What would be the practical benefits of knowing such information?

____

____

____

B. To *extrapolate* means to use one idea to understand a larger one. If one kilo of food was enough for three people, you could "extrapolate" to suggest that ten kilos would be enough for thirty people. A global positioning system (GPS) uses satellites to track one's location. Together with an accelerometer (a speed measuring device that tracks motion), an activity tracker can tell how far and how fast you go. Read this excerpt from Listening 1 and then number the activities in order of the effort required (1 = most effort; 4 = least effort).

> Those old ones [pedometers] used an internal ball mechanism that you would hear click; it would activate a switch every time you took a step. Those were essentially just step counters, so any data on distance and calories burned were just extrapolated out of the number of steps you took. The new ones use this accelerometer technology, along with GPS positioning, to figure out how much movement you're doing of any kind—are you standing, sitting, lying down, fidgeting?—along with how intensely you're exerting yourself.

_______ sitting _______ sleeping _______ standing _______ walking

C. These words and phrases will help you understand Listening 1. Read the definitions and then use each word or phrase in a sentence. Compare your sentences with a partner.

WORDS/PHRASES	DEFINITIONS	SENTENCES
1 caveats (n.)	warnings about rules or limits	
2 cumbersome (adj.)	too large or heavy to be useful	
3 discrepancy (n.)	lack of agreement between facts	
4 ICU (n.)	intensive care unit (in a hospital)	
5 longevity (n.)	long life	
6 notoriously (adv.)	widely and unfavourably; infamously	
7 obtrusive (adj.)	standing out in an unwelcome way	
8 sleep apnea (n.)	temporary pause in breathing when sleeping	
9 thermogenesis (n.)	production of heat by a human or animal body	

While You Listen

D. Listening 1 is about the different features of activity trackers. Before you listen, read the topics and predict what you think each will be about. Write brief predictions in the first column. The first time you listen to the interview, try to understand the gist. Listen a second time and take notes. Listen a third time to see what you can infer from your notes in terms of informed guesses. You will use your notes to write a summary in the Warm-Up Assignment.

TOPICS	NOTES
❶ BEYOND PEDOMETERS *how activity trackers (ATs) are better than pedometers*	• safety strap • ______ • ______ • ______
❷ ACTIVITY TRACKER DIFFERENCES	• ______ • ______ • ______ • NEAT: non-exercise activity thermogenesis • overestimates activity by ______
❸ SMARTPHONES	• ______ • ______ • drawbacks: ______ ______
❹ SLEEP QUALITY	• ______ • ______ • won't diagnose ______ • restless doesn't = ______
❺ ACCURACY	• ______ • ______ • Harvard researcher: ______
❻ EVIDENCE	• ______ • ______ • 2007 study: ______

After You Listen

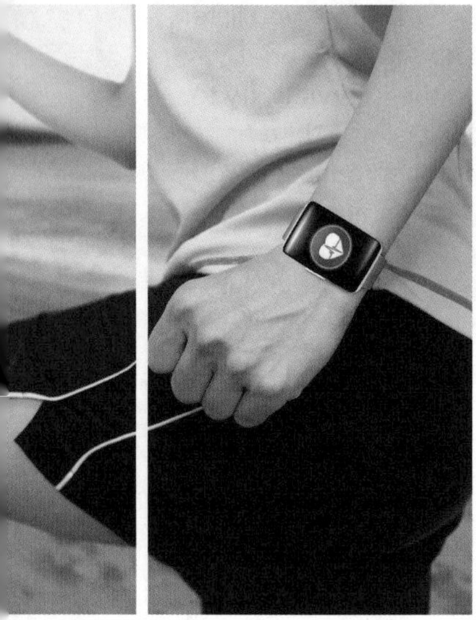

E. Answer these questions. Then, discuss with a partner.

1. Why does the interviewer think people might consider an electronic activity monitor?

2. Besides pedometers that clip to your waistband, what other ways does Basaraba say you can wear activity trackers?

3. What are some companies doing to make activity trackers more attractive?

4. What is a special advantage of the disposable activity tracker?

5. To what kinds of activity does non-exercise activity thermogenesis refer?

6. What is the main attraction of using a phone over an activity tracker?

7. What do sleep apps measure in terms of activity?

8. Why does Basaraba mention that the activity trackers do not detect sleep apnea? Make an inference.

MyBookshelf > My eLab > Exercises > Chapter 6 > Activity Trackers and Apps

Develop Your Vocabulary: When you are trying to learn a new word, use it ten or more times in your conversations and writing to help remember it.

F. Based on everything you have heard and read, work in a group to design the perfect activity tracker that includes all the features mentioned in Listening 1. Think of other features that would make it better.

FOCUS ON GRAMMAR

Conditional Sentences

Conditional sentences are used to imagine what could happen, what might have happened, and what you wish would happen. Conditional sentences generally have two parts: an *if*-clause and a result clause. This sentence, paraphrased from Listening 1, is an example of a conditional sentence:

> If you've resolved to sit less and stand more, you might consider an activity monitor.

There are three conditional forms. Read the explanations and examples to understand when and how to use them.

CONDITIONAL FORMS	USE	*IF*-CLAUSE VERB TENSE	RESULT CLAUSE VERB TENSE
FIRST CONDITIONAL	for general truths and automatic results	simple present If I **exercise**,	simple present I **am** thirsty.
	when conditions and results are real or possible	simple present If I **exercise**,	*will* + simple future I **will lose** weight.
SECOND CONDITIONAL	in present or future unreal conditions	simple past If I **exercised**,	*would* + simple present I **would be** healthier now.
THIRD CONDITIONAL	for unreal past events and hypothetical results	past perfect If I **had run** faster,	*would have* + past participle I **would have won** the race.

Use the phrases to write conditional sentences.

1. FIRST CONDITIONAL (present):
   dog listens carefully / recognizes footsteps in another room

   ____

   ____

2. FIRST CONDITIONAL (future):
   we are late / take the bus

   ____

   ____

3. SECOND CONDITIONAL:
   we improve our senses / more aware of pollution

   ____

   ____

4. THIRD CONDITIONAL:
   people developed a dog's hearing / their brains adapted

   ____

   ____

Use what you learned about conditional sentences when you prepare assignments.

MyBookshelf > My eLab > Exercises > Chapter 6 > Grammar Review

LISTENING 2

Our Better Selves

Mikhail Bulgakov's (1891–1940) satirical 1925 novel *Heart of a Dog*, tells the story of a stray dog that is given human organs and certain injections and develops into a beastly man. Today, scientists are active in research to give humans biological and technological enhancements that are common among animals. While we might eventually extend our abilities and senses, we might also find that our changes in perceptions affect the ways we think, perhaps altering what it means to be human. Listening 2 reflects on what having the sensory abilities of different animals might be like.

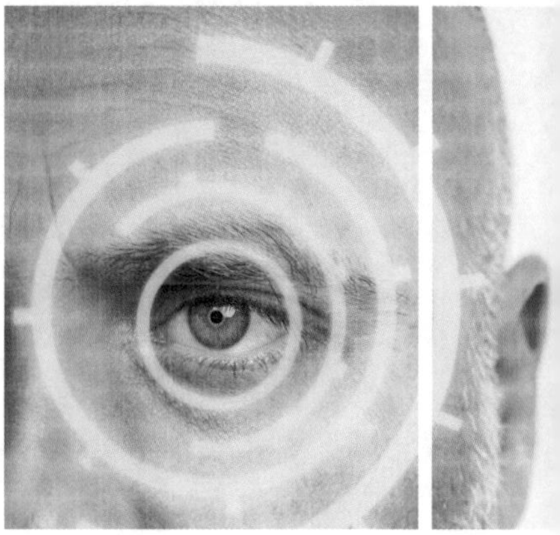

VOCABULARY BUILD

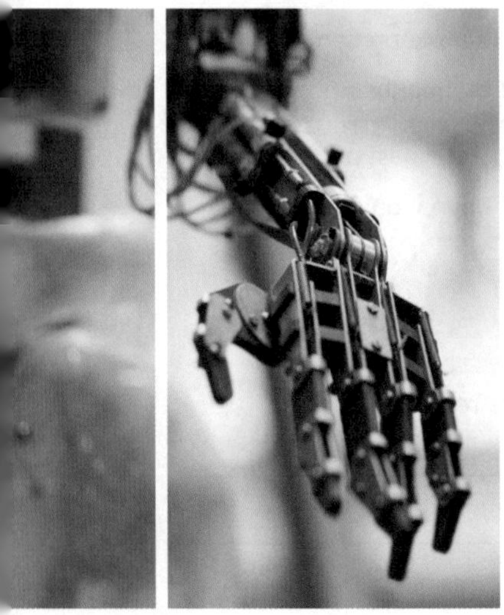

In the following exercises, explore key words from Listening 2.

A. Fill in the blanks with the correct words to complete the paragraph. Use a dictionary for words you don't understand.

frontier	further	overwhelming	restrict	trigger

Recently, there has been an ____________________ interest among people wanting to go ____________________ than just correcting disabilities. However, some worry that this might ____________________ a race among militaries to build soldiers with enhanced abilities. For this reason, many consider that governments should ____________________ research in these areas. Otherwise, we will enter a new ____________________ where humans and soldiers are separate species.

B. Choose the word that best completes each sentence. Key words are in bold.

1. Because the building was **upgraded**, everything worked (better / worse).
2. The evolutionary **adaptation** of (decreased / improved) vision helped the eagle to hunt.
3. In trying to **discriminate** between different sounds, the dog can identify (differences / similarities).
4. In terms of **enhancements**, most people would prefer (improved / reduced) vision.
5. When he talked about a **spectrum** of enhancement opportunities, he was referring to the (colours / range).

C. VOCABULARY EXTENSION**:** The *re-* prefix in the word *restrict* means "again" or "back." Write a definition for each of these *re-* words from Listening 2.

1. reactions (n.): ________________________________
2. regain (v.): ________________________________

3. relies (v.): ______________________________

4. replace (v.): ______________________________

5. repositioning (v.): ______________________________

6. research (n.): ______________________________

D. These words and phrases will help you understand Listening 2. Choose the best definition for each.

1	acutely	a) intensely	b) attractively
2	prosthesis	a) sports essay	b) artificial limb
3	infrared	a) invisible light emitted by heated objects	b) colour popular in the fashion industry
4	pattern recognition	a) computer function for mapping data	b) computer function for mapping camouflage
5	differently abled	a) with physical or mental challenges	b) with enhanced abilities
6	spectrum	a) rainbow or other light system	b) range of degrees
7	speculative	a) imagining without a basis in knowledge	b) creating or improving one's vision
8	ultraviolet light	a) type of blue radiation used in the creation of food colours	b) invisible form of light that, in excess, can cause cancer

Before You Listen

A. Write some ways in which people currently try to improve their health and fitness. Which do you think are the most effective? Discuss in a group.

____

____

B. Speculation—imagining the future—plays a large part in Listening 2. Read this excerpt and then write other tools we already use that extend our senses and abilities. Discuss your answers with a partner.

> But today, I'd like to branch out from the practical to the speculative and engage you with a number of "what if" questions to do with enhancing your senses. Of course, we can already enhance our senses with technology. For example, we can see both farther *and* closer with binoculars and microscopes. We can use microphones to hear the faintest sounds across great distances. We have machines in development that can smell cancer in a person and others that can analyze textures too fine for a finger to distinguish. But what if some of these technologies could be incorporated directly into the human body?

____

____

____

While You Listen

C. In her lecture, Dr. Morris talks about several creatures with different sensory abilities (vision, hearing, smell, taste, touch). Before you listen, reflect on what you already know about the senses of each creature. The first time you listen, take notes on each creature's abilities. Listen a second time to fill in details. Listen a third time to check your notes.

	CREATURES	NOTES
	EAGLES 	With an eagle's vision, you could read the small print on a newspaper from 30 metres
ELEPHANTS 	PIGEONS 	
CATS 	MOTHS 	
	DOGS 	
	AFRICAN RATS 	
	JEWEL BEETLES 	
	MOLES 	

After You Listen

D. Indicate whether these statements are true or false, according to the listening.

STATEMENTS	TRUE	FALSE
❶ There are machines in development to smell cancer.	☐	☐
❷ People already have binoculars and microscopes in their bodies.	☐	☐
❸ Cochlear implants are used to enhance a person's hearing.	☐	☐
❹ Dr. Morris was called "eagle-eyed" by her father.	☐	☐
❺ Most people would have an operation if it would give them an eagle's peripheral vision.	☐	☐
❻ Hearing dozens of conversations is something people already do.	☐	☐
❼ Artists have a greater awareness of colour than non-artists.	☐	☐
❽ A mole uses its sense of smell to detect earthworms.	☐	☐

E. Answer these questions. Then, discuss with a partner.

1. If you could choose to improve one sense, which one would it be? Why? In your answer, reference Dr. Morris's speech.

___

___

___

2. Why might having eagle eyes influence your thinking? How would this happen?

___

___

___

3. Why does Dr. Morris think better hearing might make a more polite society? Do you agree or disagree? Explain why.

___

___

___

___

___

!

Pronunciation: Sometimes, "the" is pronounced "thee" (to indicate it's the only one) and "a" is pronounced "eh" to indicate a particular one. Use these pronunciations for emphasis.

4. Dr. Morris suggests that better senses might make us a more caring species. What does she mean by this? Do you agree or disagree? Explain why.

____

____

____

____

MyBookshelf > My eLab > Exercises > Chapter 6 > Our Better Selves

Academic Survival Skill

Paraphrasing and Summarizing

An important comprehension and study skill is discussing lectures and other types of talks (e.g., debates, interviews, speeches) after you listen to them. Discussing a lecture helps you to check whether you understood the information exactly as others did and to figure out the answers to any questions you might have had. Discussions also help you to reinforce the ideas.

Paraphrasing

One technique for capturing ideas when you listen is to paraphrase. When you paraphrase, look for the main ideas and write or say them in your own words. Start by considering what information is unessential.

A. Read this excerpt from Listening 2. Cross out the unnecessary words.

> If you implanted eagle eyes, how would it influence your thinking? You would certainly take in far greater quantities of information. Would your brain be able to process it? I would say yes; the brain is a very flexible organ. Your awareness—and I suppose your interest—in the world would increase. Artists, for example, have a greater awareness and memory for colour than non-artists.

B. Use the main ideas that you were left with in task A to write a one-sentence paraphrase of the paragraph. Compare your paraphrase with a partner's.

____

____

____

Summarizing

Summarizing is not just a skill you use *after* listening; it's best to mentally summarize *while* you listen. When you hear the title or topic sentence of a presentation, you begin to get an idea of what it is about and can then choose an appropriate graphic organizer to help you summarize the ideas. You could choose a timeline for a discussion of events or a flow chart for a talk about a process. While you continue to listen, adjust your mental summary by modifying what you think based on the new information you hear.

After you listen, it's easier to summarize based on notes you took while you listened. When you summarize, stick to the main points and try to identify the argument or thesis in what you heard.

C. Choose the best summary of Listening 2. Then, write an explanation of what makes it superior to the others.

- ☐ Seeing like an eagle or having a mole's sense of touch would require impractical surgical procedures that would turn people into freaks.
- ☐ Various creatures have enhanced or different senses that many people some day may be able to adopt but which might change the way they think.
- ☐ Understanding the world from another creature's point of view would not be worth the difficulty of adopting one or more new senses.

____

____

WARM-UP ASSIGNMENT

Summarize an Interview

In this Warm-Up Assignment, you will write a summary of Listening 1 and then present it to a group of classmates.

A. Review the notes you took for Listening 1 and the answers you wrote to the questions in task E (page 124).

B. Use this information to write a one-paragraph summary. Apply what you learned about summarizing in Academic Survival Skill. Write at least one conditional sentence (see Focus on Grammar, page 125).

C. Convert your notes to a graphic organizer such as a flow chart, mind map, or timeline. Use your graphic organizer when you present your summary to your group.

D. Form groups of six, and present your summary to your group members.

E. When all group members have presented, ask for feedback on how you could improve your summary, graphic organizer, and presentation.

LISTENING 3

VIDEO

The Future of Human Enhancements

We all enhance ourselves in small ways, including wearing glasses to see better and putting on running shoes that make us faster. These enhancements are accepted, but people question biological enhancements that may give some advantages over others, such as transplanted organs that are superior to normal ones. When these become available, should they first only be available to the wealthy?

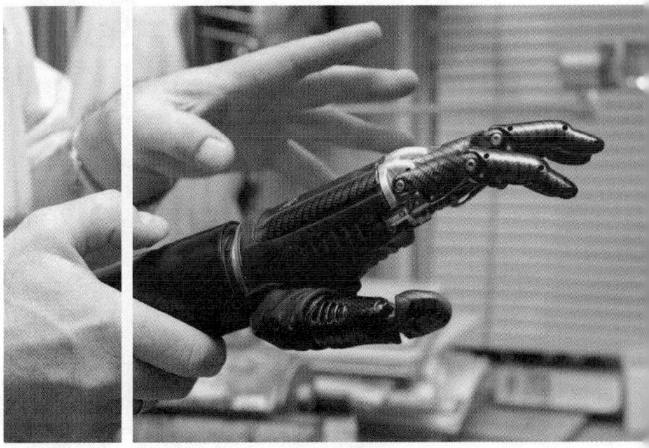

VOCABULARY BUILD

In the following exercises, explore key words from Listening 3.

A. Write the key word next to its definition.

cognitive	distinction	equitable	extinct	radical

DEFINITION	KEY WORD
1 fair to everyone	
2 describing a large and unexpected change	
3 the mental process of learning	
4 an important difference	
5 no longer in existence	

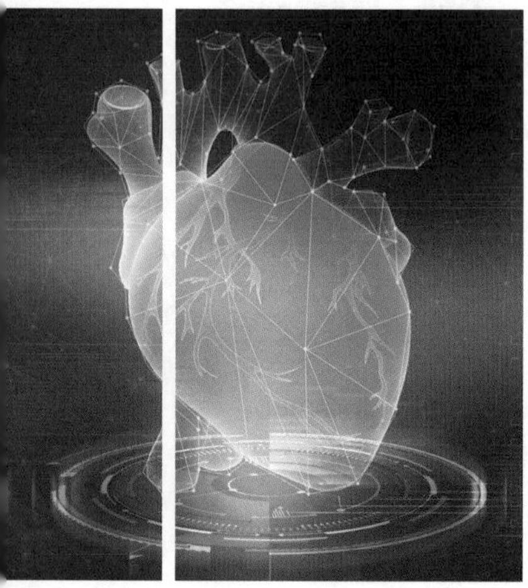

B. Draw an arrow (↓) to indicate where in each sentence the word or phrase in parentheses should be placed.

1. (**evaluating**) By all the options , we decided the first one was the best.
2. (**ancestors**) Once she started looking at all her , she realized that certain diseases were common in her family.
3. (**evolution**) A basic principle in is that better adapted species survive.
4. (**anchors**) He his ideas on his beliefs rather than in facts.
5. (**scenario**) She imagined a in which she could change her eyes to see great distances.

C. These technical words and idiomatic phrases will help you understand Listening 3. Match each to its definition.

KEY WORDS AND PHRASES		DEFINITIONS
1 anaesthesia	______	a) genetic similarities to one's ancestors
2 connect the dots	______	b) cells descended from other cells
3 DNA inheritance	______	c) a disease that affects the liver
4 gamma rays	______	d) a weakening and wasting of the muscles
5 germline	______	e) a parasite that lives under the skin
6 Guinea worm	______	f) a course of actions that can lead to disaster

KEY WORDS AND PHRASES		DEFINITIONS
7 hepatitis virus	________	g) a bacterium, virus, or microscopic organism that causes disease
8 leap of faith	________	h) insensitivity to pain, such as through drugs during surgery
9 muscular dystrophy	________	i) disease of the nervous system that causes paralysis
10 pathogen	________	j) a belief in something without proof
11 polio	________	k) put ideas together
12 slippery slope	________	l) electromagnetic radiation

MyBookshelf > My eLab > Exercises > Chapter 6 > Vocabulary Review

Before You Listen

A. Read George Church's introduction to his speech. Why do you think he makes his point about *not* advocating something?

> So, I just want to point out that Jaime and I are tasked with creating a realistic vision of the future enhancements, and whenever I'm asked that, [...] I feel I have to point out that, when a scientist describes what could happen or answers a question from a journalist about what could happen, that doesn't mean that they're advocating that happening. So, just please keep that in mind. I will make futuristic statements.

____

____

____

B. Church mentions examples of technological, cultural, and biological enhancements. Write an example for each one, and, after listening, check to see if your ideas are similar to the ones mentioned in the lecture.

TECHNOLOGICAL: ____

CULTURAL: ____

BIOLOGICAL: ____

While You Listen

C. While you watch, use the prompts to take notes on the key points. Watch again and fill in details. You will use your notes to write a summary for discussion in the Final Assignment.

PROMPTS	DETAILS
1 We take science fiction, we	

PROMPTS	DETAILS
❷ And so, when we have any new therapy, any new technology, we have	
❸ For example,	*FDA, EMA, CFDA*
❹ There are certain things they are not tasked to do, typically	
❺ They do not consider long-term effects of	
❻ They do not consider	
❼ And they don't worry too much about	*e.g., 32-ounce sugary drinks*
❽ Nevertheless, we accept the radical enhancements on	
❾ And I think we draw too much of a distinction between	*e.g., mobile phone*
❿ But what are examples of enhancement?	*e.g., people having blond hair and blue eyes threatening society*
⓫ Most of the things that are enhancements that are inherited are physics and chemistry,	*e.g., super-athletes versus*
⓬ We can see the entire spectrum from	
⓭ We talk about some of the exceptional people in the world that are like, in a certain sense, naturally enhanced,	*e.g.,*
⓮ I think we're mainly concerned about	
⓯ It's okay for us to be enhanced relative to	*e.g., we don't worry about smallpox; it's equitably distributed*
⓰ So, we don't have to worry about the costs of distributing and	

PROMPTS	DETAILS
17 We're still worrying about that with	
18 We're almost done with	
19 And that's an enhancement ... that gives us	
20 If we come up with an adult enhancement, that can spread	
21 Cultural evolution and cultural spread is so much	
22 I think one of the possibilities that we can't do with the machines necessarily already ... is	
23 We aim for being a new normal or just normal, and we	*e.g., muscular dystrophy, cognitive decline*
24 Another example is organ transplants: we recently made some	
25 If you're going to transplant an organ, you might want that organ to be	
26 And so, you might want that organ to not get	
27 So, you might want that organ to be resistant to	*pathogens*
28 You might want them to be resistant to	
29 So, you might want alternatives to anaesthesia or to the kinds of drugs that ... reduce pain but are	
30 There are humans that actually have chronic	
31 This is a genetic problem they have, but imagine ...	

After You Listen

D. Answer each question, and then discuss your answers with a partner to see if you agree.

1. What does Church mean when he says that his lab turns science fiction into science fact?

   ____

   ____

2. Why is international equitable access to new developments important?

   ____

   ____

3. International monitoring organizations do not consider the long-term effects of technology. What is a negative consequence of everyone having mobile phones?

   ____

   ____

4. How are mobile phones an example of cultural DNA just because family members all have them?

   ____

   ____

5. What is the example of the car meant to explain?

   ____

   ____

6. The mention of everyone having blond hair and blue eyes, for example, is meant to suggest that, if we have access to enhancements, everyone will want the same things. Do you agree? Why or why not?

   ____

   ____

7. Why is cultural evolution faster than biological evolution?

   ____

   ____

8. What are the consequences of overshooting when developing treatments to slow cognitive decline?

   ____

   ____

E. Church mentions Helen Keller and Stephen Hawking, who he says are examples of people with enhanced abilities, both making up for physical limitations. Think of three people with enhanced abilities, and explain their abilities.

After, discuss with a partner whether you would want each ability. Why or why not?

PEOPLE	ABILITIES
❶	
❷	
❸	

F. At the end of his speech, Church combines a fact with a thought experiment: "There are humans that actually have chronic insensitivity to pain. This is a genetic problem they have, but imagine you could turn that on and off." In a group, discuss the positive and negative consequences of being able to turn pain on and off.

MyBookshelf > My eLab > Exercises > Chapter 6 > The Future of Human Enhancements

FOCUS ON SPEAKING

Speaking with Aids

When you listen to a lecture, it is natural to remember more if the speaker uses aids. This is because the information will be stored in different parts of your brain associated with vision, hearing, and language. Such aids come in many forms, including physical objects (called *props*), visual aids like computer presentations, interactive graphics (e.g., charts that change on the screen), photos, illustrations, and graphic organizers. Audio segments and video clips are also useful aids.

A. Imagine you are giving a presentation on activity trackers. Number these aids in terms of how effective you think each would be in helping your listeners to remember the content of your talk (1 = most helpful; 7 = least helpful).

_______ audience volunteer helping you demonstrate an activity tracker

_______ audio recording of a favourable testimonial from an activity tracker user

_______ chart showing an increase in the number of activity tracker users by month

_______ interactive graphics showing weight loss

_______ speaking on your own, without any aids

_______ text-only computer presentations

_______ video of a person using an activity tracker throughout the day

Among the most popular visual aids are computer presentations. The individual screens of a computer presentation are called *slides* and the collection is called a *deck*. When creating a deck, consider these points:

- Use large, readable text, but keep it to a minimum: use phrases, not full sentences.
- Make sure your slides are readable, particularly the charts and diagrams. Simplify them to only include essential information.

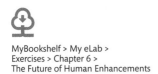

- Use slides to make your audience think; include questions on the slides and provide explanations as you talk.
- Use colours and memorable images to capture attention and to support your message. Avoid humour or other elements that might distract.
- When you present, never face the screen while you are speaking and don't read from it. The audience can read faster than you can speak, so add to what you have written with new information.
- Include one or two slides per minute of the lecture: too many slides lead to confusion and too few lead to boredom.

MyBookshelf > My eLab > Exercises > Chapter 6 > Focus on Speaking

B. With a partner, discuss these three computer presentation slides about motivation. Which would make the greatest impact in your presentation?

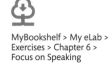

Winston Churchill said, "If you're going through hell, keep going."

Why?

motivation (n.): reason or reasons one has for acting or behaving in a particular way

FINAL ASSIGNMENT

Summarize a Lecture and Participate in a Group Discussion

Use what you learned in this chapter to take part in a group discussion of the lecture you heard in Listening 3.

A. Prepare for the discussion by writing a summary of the lecture using the notes you took for Listening 3. If you refer to the lecture, make sure you paraphrase. Apply what you learned about paraphrasing and summarizing in Academic Survival Skill (page 130). Write at least one conditional sentence (see Focus on Grammar, page 125).

___

___

___

B. On a separate page, prepare a graphic organizer, such as a flow chart, mind map, or timeline, to support your summary.

C. Write three questions you would like to discuss about something you heard in the lecture. For example: would people want to know if others had been enhanced in some way, and what would they do with such information?

1. ___
2. ___
3. ___

D. Form a group of six and begin the discussion. During the discussion, share your summary and your graphic organizer and ask your questions. Take notes on other students' ideas. At the end, summarize what the group discussed using one visual aid (see Focus on Speaking, page 137). For example, you could use a computer-aided presentation and include the main points, possibly using a graphic organizer.

E. Choose one group member to present the summary of your discussion to the rest of the class.

F. When all groups have presented, ask for feedback on how you could improve your presentation.

How confident are you?

Think about what you learned in this chapter. Use the table to decide what you should review.

I LEARNED ...	I AM CONFIDENT	I NEED TO REVIEW
vocabulary related to health and fitness;	☐	☐
to predict and infer ideas;	☐	☐
how to use thought experiments to explore ideas;	☐	☐
about conditional sentences;	☐	☐
how to paraphrase and summarize;	☐	☐
to summarize an interview;	☐	☐
to use aids when speaking;	☐	☐
to summarize a lecture and participate in a group discussion.	☐	☐

CHAPTER 7

New Ways to Learn

Summerhill, a British school founded in 1921, made class attendance voluntary and gave every teacher and student an equal vote in all decisions. Countless other educational experiments have sought better ways to teach and learn. Recently, technology has changed the nature of schools, partly reflecting the shift from traditional jobs requiring manual labour to new jobs that set thinking skills as a priority. In some educational contexts, the computer has become an interactive tutor, replacing the teacher, while other schools have gone in the opposite direction, rejecting technology and returning to traditional classroom practices.

What do you think is the best way to learn?

In this chapter, you will

- learn vocabulary related to new ways of learning;
- listen for processes;
- organize ideas into a sequence;
- review gerunds and infinitives;
- enhance your message with non-verbal communication;
- start a discussion with a thesis statement;
- give a process presentation and explain it in a seminar.

GEARING UP

A. Look at this illustration of a traditional classroom and then answer the questions.

An 1845 magazine illustration of a Paris classroom

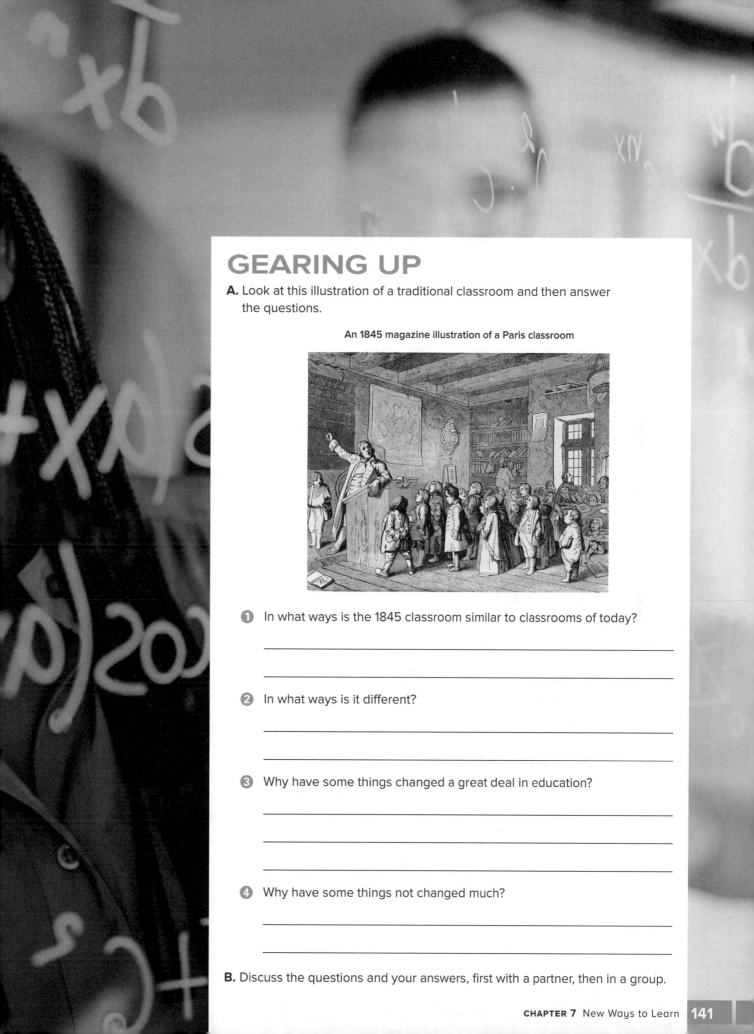

1. In what ways is the 1845 classroom similar to classrooms of today?

____

____

2. In what ways is it different?

____

____

3. Why have some things changed a great deal in education?

____

____

____

4. Why have some things not changed much?

____

____

B. Discuss the questions and your answers, first with a partner, then in a group.

VOCABULARY BUILD OVERVIEW

Below are the key words you will practise in this chapter. Check the words you understand, then underline the words you use. Highlight the words you need to learn.

New Learning

nouns

appreciation*
apprenticeships
ambitions
assumption*
avalanche
collaboration
elements*
ethics*
ideology*
incentive*
independence
liberal arts*
mechanics*
personalization
perspective*
pillars
simulation*

verbs

advocate*
concentrate*
disconnecting
entailed
foster
incorporates*
react*
self-orient*

adjectives

classic*
sensitive
specific*

* Appears on the Academic Word List

FOCUS ON LISTENING

Listening for Processes

Every time you follow a recipe, you are completing a process. When speakers talk about processes, they use a range of verb tenses and key words that mark stages in a sequence: *before*, *during*, and *after*. Processes are also often marked by ordinal numbers: *first*, *second*, *third*. When you listen to a process, focus on the tenses and key words to understand the sequence.

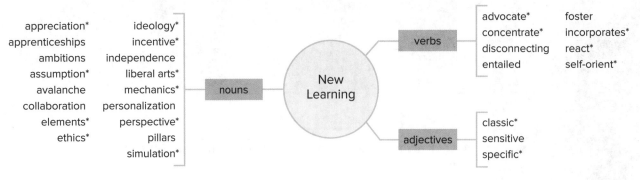

A. Processes involve steps over time. In some processes, time is indicated by changes in tense. Number the following phrases to indicate when they occur in time from first (1) to last (5).

_______ I will have bought a book.

_______ I bought a book.

_______ I will be buying a book.

_______ I was buying a book.

_______ I am buying a book.

B. Read an excerpt from Listening 1. Highlight the verbs and two expressions that show time. With a partner, discuss how the sentence describes a process.

> I've had a couple of students, who after I've given them the speech at the beginning about starting out at an F, who have dropped out, but once the class gets going, I have discovered that ..., that they get into it pretty quickly.

____

____

____

____

C. The following are words you will hear when people talk about processes. Use a dictionary to look up any you don't know. Then underline the correct words to complete each sentence in the paragraph.

after	later	now	sometimes	until
always	meanwhile	once	soon	when
during	never	simultaneously	subsequently	whenever
earlier	next	so far	then	while

(Soon / When) you want to teach yourself a new process, you can use online videos. (Sometimes / During) you will quickly find something useful. (Once / Meanwhile) you do, you can watch it several times. You can also go back to it (subsequently / whenever) you forget part of a process. (Simultaneously / Until) you have mastered it, keep trying!

FOCUS ON CRITICAL THINKING

Organizing Ideas into a Sequence

The Latin term *non sequitur* describes a comment that doesn't follow from a previous statement or idea. It's confusing when speakers go off topic, and their listeners are likely to lose interest in the topic and respect for the speaker. When you explain a topic that is complicated, it's necessary to organize it both for yourself and for your listeners. The most common approaches to do so are as a process, in chronological order, or in order of importance. Understanding each approach helps you identify and better understand other speakers.

A **process order** shows things in a logical sequence, often because steps must be done in a particular order. For example, with a recipe, you must wash and chop vegetables before cooking them. Similarly, explaining cause and effect often involves a process. Use a flow chart to organize your ideas about a process.

A. Read the paragraph and write the process in a flow chart.

The speakers will introduce themselves and their schools and then give brief explanations of the merits of their personal approaches to education. After, I'll ask them to discuss the commonalities.

• *introduce selves* →	→	→	

Chronological order explains a sequence that happens over time. A chronological order could happen over a few seconds, such as when describing a car accident, or over centuries, such as when describing climate change events. Use a timeline to organize your ideas about a process.

B. Read the paragraph and put the events in order on the timeline.

Once you have built your own canoe, paddled it for a week, hiked another week through winter snows to climb a mountain range, and then made your way back to base camp, you have the confidence to do anything.

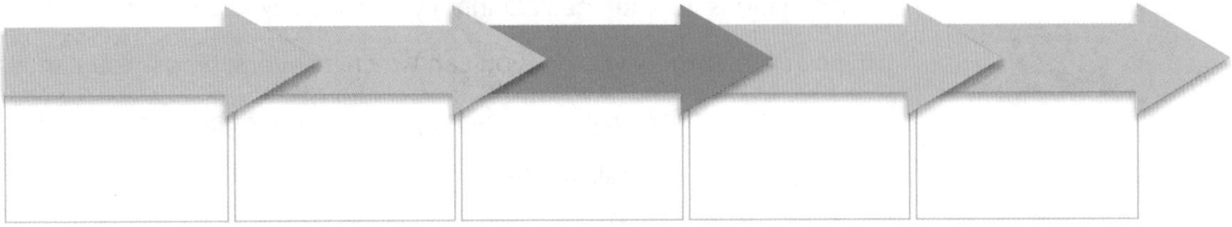

Order of importance organizes ideas based on which is more, most, and least important. Order of importance can be used two ways: The most important idea can be said first, followed by supporting ideas, or supporting details can lead up to the most important idea. Use bullet points to order a main important point, and indent supporting points.

C. Read the paragraph and highlight the most important sentence.

Our only rule is that each day and each project have to be fuelled by passion. We embrace dreamers because they are the ones who are going to change the world. These dreamers come to our program and are called partners—it says that on the business card they each receive the first day. "Partner." They decide on their projects and responsibilities. The struggle of sorting out who does what is an important part of their growth. If a team is designing an application that will save thousands of lives, someone still needs to take out the garbage.

LISTENING 1

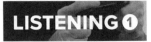

Gamification

Beyond entertainment, games for the young are often about learning skills that will be useful later in life. Today, many video games teach competitive and collaborative strategies, political systems, and money management. Could games be used to improve the teaching of subjects in a university context? Listening 1 explores this question in an interview with Professor Lee Sheldon, who talks about how he uses game-based learning in his classes.

VOCABULARY BUILD

In the following exercises, explore key words from Listening 1.

A. Fill in the blanks with the correct words to complete the paragraph. Use a dictionary to look up words you don't understand.

ethics	incentive	incorporates	react	specific

Do you need an __________________ to behave well? A society generally __________________ a set of beliefs about how people should behave. We call this set of beliefs __________________, and these are built around how the society views __________________ problems. Sometimes a society faces a new problem, and an individual has to __________________ in a way that considers how the set of beliefs applies.

B. Choose the word or phrase that best completes each sentence. Key words are in bold.

1. It's often necessary to **concentrate** on the small details of a problem.
   a) ponder b) improve c) focus
2. There are many **elements** that go into making a classroom successful.
   a) parts b) hot points c) chemicals
3. A board game **simulation** of a stock market won't involve real money.
   a) investment b) introduction c) imitation
4. Traditional **mechanics** may not have the skills to repair new cars' electric systems.
   a) robots b) repair personnel c) computers
5. Through **collaboration**, students can learn from each other.
   a) competition b) absence c) teamwork

C. These words and phrases will help you understand Listening 1. Choose the best definition for each.

1. attrition — a) gradually reducing strength — b) identifying a location
2. avatars — a) blue aliens — b) online representations of a person
3. buzzword — a) language of bees — b) fashionable phrase
4. clunky — a) awkward and outdated — b) sound of a broken wheel
5. run of the mill — a) ordinary — b) unordinary
6. sage on the stage — a) teacher-centred — b) learner-centred
7. spiff up — a) make less attractive — b) make more attractive

!

Develop Your Vocabulary: Try learning one new word each day. Keep a notebook or online file where you list the word, its definition, and an example sentence. Review frequently.

Before You Listen

A. One focus of Listening 1 is the idea of motivation. Motivation is usually either *intrinsic* (based on personal interest or desires) or *extrinsic* (based on external pressures). For example, students may play a game for pure enjoyment (intrinsic) or because their teacher directs them to do so (extrinsic). Write three things you do that are intrinsically motivated and three that are extrinsically motivated.

INTRINSICALLY MOTIVATED	EXTRINSICALLY MOTIVATED
❶	❶
❷	❷
❸	❸

B. Read this excerpt from Listening 1. Then, in a group, discuss which features of a video game might be included when designing a new way to teach various subjects.

> Well, a lot of kids—and probably a few adults—wore their thumbs red playing *Super Mario Brothers*, and, while video games are spectacularly successful as home entertainment, some hope games can equally engage students as learning tools. Today, as part of our project By Design, we were looking at designing a curriculum that incorporates gaming. The buzzword in education is "gamification"; the students are studying game design and taking a course from one of gamification's pioneers.

While You Listen

C. Listening 1 gives perspectives on a course based on gaming principles. The first time you listen, try to understand the gist. Listen a second time and complete the notes.

SPEAKERS	NOTES
Anna Maria Tremonti	• games can equally engage students as ________ • students studying game design course from gamification pioneer
Student 1	• we had to make a story of ________
Student 2	• competing with classmates is ________
Student 1	• incentive/motivation – short-term and long-term ________ – not motivated by ________
Lee Sheldon	• gamification = ________ • aka: ________
	• you start class with an F but can ________ • class is designed as a game: *competition + collaboration* • apply gaming principles ________

SPEAKERS	NOTES
Lee Sheldon	• not letter grades: ____________________
	• complete a quest or craft something = ____________________
	• research (questing) to take exams: ____________________
	• ____________________
	• ____________________
	• teaching like this since 2008
	• class maps game terminology *onto game-related activities*
	• activities have ____________________
	• added ____________________
	• benefits:
	– grades: ____________________
	– attendance ____________________
	– make up ____________________
	– intrinsic rather than ____________________
	– extrinsic rewards = ____________________

After You Listen

D. Review your notes and number these sentences in the correct order to form a summary of Listening 1.

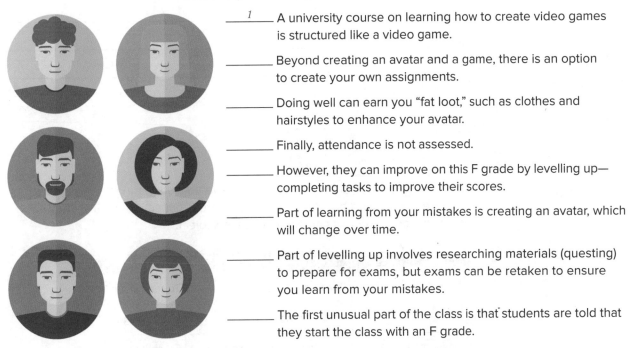

___*1*___ A university course on learning how to create video games is structured like a video game.

________ Beyond creating an avatar and a game, there is an option to create your own assignments.

________ Doing well can earn you "fat loot," such as clothes and hairstyles to enhance your avatar.

________ Finally, attendance is not assessed.

________ However, they can improve on this F grade by levelling up—completing tasks to improve their scores.

________ Part of learning from your mistakes is creating an avatar, which will change over time.

________ Part of levelling up involves researching materials (questing) to prepare for exams, but exams can be retaken to ensure you learn from your mistakes.

________ The first unusual part of the class is that students are told that they start the class with an F grade.

E. Answer the following questions and then discuss your answers with a partner.

1. What is surprising about gamification as an approach?

____

2. Why is attendance so high in this course compared to other courses?

____

____

3. Why does the teacher let the students repeat the exam as often as they like?

____

____

4. What other subjects are being taught using gamification?

____

____

5. Why do students enter the class with an F grade?

____

____

6. Why does the teacher use gamification rather than a traditional approach?

____

____

7. The Holocaust—the Nazis' murder of millions during WWII—is not a light-hearted topic. What might be the pros and cons of teaching serious topics as games? Discuss in a group.

____

____

____

____

MyBookshelf > My eLab > Exercises > Chapter 7 > Gamification

FOCUS ON GRAMMAR

Gerunds and Infinitives

When you listened to Listening 1, you may have noticed gerunds, the *-ing* form of the verb. *Gerunds* and *infinitives* are verb forms that act like nouns. They can be the subject, object, or complement of the subject.

PART OF SENTENCE	GERUND	INFINITIVE
subject	**Reading** is fun.	**To read** is fun.*
object	I like **reading**.	I like **to read**.
complement	Something I love is **reading**.	Something I love is **to read**.

*Expressions using the infinitive as the subject are considered formal and uncommon in casual speech and writing.

▶

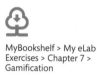

Gerunds and infinitives can also have subjects and objects:

Reading **a book** is fun. I like to read **a book**.

Like other nouns, gerunds (but not infinitives) can be modified by adjectives:

Bedtime reading is fun.

In some cases, such as with the verb *like*, you can use either a gerund or an infinitive. However, sometimes the choice of a gerund or an infinitive depends on the main verb of the sentence. There are many gerunds and infinitives; pay attention when you listen and read to learn when to use each one. Here are some rules and commonly used gerunds and infinitives.

Use a gerund:

- When you use a form of *go* with sporting activities and pastimes:

  She **went** *swimming*. He **goes** *shopping*.

- After a preposition, as the object:

  We'll eat **before** *starting* our homework.

- When you use expressions with *have*, *spend*, and *waste*:

  We **spent** the day *reading*. I **wasted** my time *sleeping*.

- When you describe a concrete action:

  I **like** *teaching*.

Use an infinitive:

- When you show intention or purpose:

  I **want** *to teach*. I **will** study *to improve*.

- When you show a reason:

  We **were glad** *to see* their progress.

- When you talk about a general or possible action:

  I **would like** *to learn*.

- When the verb is followed by a pronoun or noun referring to a person:

  I asked **him** *to study*.

A. These verbs are usually followed by a gerund. Write sentences for each combination of verbs. Use any tense for the first verb, and change the second verb into a gerund.

1. appreciate + see: *I appreciate seeing old friends.*
2. complete + watch: ____________________
3. discuss + donate: ____________________
4. involve + try: ____________________
5. suggest + find: ____________________

____

▶

Use what you learned about gerunds and infinitives when you prepare assignments.

MyBookshelf > My eLab > Exercises > Chapter 7 > Grammar Review

B. These verbs are usually followed by an infinitive. Write sentences for each combination of verbs. Use any tense for the first verb, and change the second verb into an infinitive.

1. agree + fight: *The group agreed to fight the new proposal.*
2. decide + move: ______
3. learn + program: ______
4. need + repeat: ______
5. plan + arrive: ______

FOCUS ON SPEAKING

Enhancing Your Message with Non-Verbal Communication

Why is it you sometimes have difficulty understanding what people mean when they text or phone? The problem may have to do with a lack of visual clues: facial expressions and body language. When you speak, you use a mixture of posture (how you stand), facial expressions, and hand gestures.

A. Look at these different facial expressions and hand gestures. Then, write the idea or emotion that the man is trying to express in each. Compare answers with a partner.

IDEA OR EMOTION EXPRESSED

1. ______ 2. ______ 3. ______
4. ______ 5. ______ 6. ______
7. ______ 8. ______ 9. ______

B. Practise reading this excerpt from Listening 1 with a partner. The first time, read it aloud with no expressions or gestures. Without looking at the words, try saying it a second time with facial expressions and gestures; it does not matter if you do not capture the exact words.

When speaking, be careful of your hand gestures; what is common in one culture may be rude in another.

> So, my character ... , her name was Hipster, and her backstory is that she grew up in this island, her mom and dad were mechanics or engineers, and other people made up their avatars and you need to create a story to intermix them together. I was like the mechanic, someone else was a thief, and someone else was a whatever, and then we had to make a story of how they work together and how they met each other, and that was what we built upon.

MyBookshelf > My eLab > Exercises > Chapter 7 > Focus on Speaking

C. Discuss how your presentation with facial expressions and gestures added to the message you were trying to share.

LISTENING 2 VIDEO

New Models for Education

More than 100 million people each year use Khan Academy, an online video-based learning platform for a wide range of educational courses. Founder Sal Khan says that his goal is to provide a world-class education for anyone, anywhere. For his work, he has been called a superstar teacher. However, surprisingly, Khan has no background in education. Since 2016, the Khan Lab School has looked at ways to change classroom education.

VOCABULARY BUILD

In the following exercises, explore key words from Listening 2.

A. Highlight the word in parentheses that best completes each sentence. Key words are in bold.

1. In order to **foster** creativity, teachers give students (problem-solving tasks / standardized tests).
2. The idea of **apprenticeships** is to allow students to learn (after / while) they work.
3. Students have a habit of **disconnecting** from their studies when they're (too tired / wide awake).
4. One way to **self-orient** yourself to the university campus is to (take a guided tour / wander around).
5. The aim of **personalization** is to make learning more about (all students / each student).

B. Choose the best definition for each key word. Use a dictionary to check your answers.

❶ **ambitions**	a) penalties	b) desires	c) duties
❷ **pillars**	a) tablets	b) arches	c) supports
❸ **entailed**	a) involved	b) rejected	c) placed
❹ **perspective**	a) illusion	b) viewpoint	c) mirror-like
❺ **independence**	a) solitude	b) challenged	c) freedom

C. It's common to overuse certain words; most people are unaware when they do so. For example, over the course of 333 words, Yazid Arifi uses the adverb *basically* twelve times. For the sample sentence, write three words he could use instead of *basically*.

So, we **basically** don't rank the ways of learning from the most desirable one to the least [desirable] one.

ALTERNATIVES: ______________________________

Before You Listen

A. Khan Academy offers instructional videos on math and other subjects that let students learn at their own pace, spending more time on topics they find difficult and progressing more quickly on those they find easy. Would this work as well in the classroom as it does for students working alone online? Why or why not? Discuss with a partner.

B. The Khan Lab aims to challenge school artifacts (ways of doing things) and reimagine education. What are three things that should change about education and three things that should remain the same?

THINGS THAT SHOULD CHANGE	THINGS THAT SHOULD REMAIN THE SAME

While You Listen

C. The idea of Khan Labs is to investigate different ways to teach students. While you watch, fill in the notes on the key points so you can identify processes after.

KEY POINTS	EXAMPLES/EXPLANATIONS
❶ Khan Academy: __________ million users online	• operating in ________ countries
❷ founded Khan Lab School in __________	• changing schools • __________________ education
❸ Pillar 1: content __________ and self-paced	• guide themselves • online __________________
❹ Pillar 2: content __________	• self-management • time management • __________________ • __________________
❺ Pillar 3: content __________ learning	• not memorization
❻ independent study	• elementary school __________ of time • high school __________ of time
❼ personalization in education	• not directed by __________________ • children able to __________________ • people help __________________ • students can learn __________________ • or they can have formal learning
❽ promote the interactions between children and __________	• interests • imagination • __________________
❾ personalization	• self-paced • responsible for __________________ • avoid isolated students • promote __________________ • negotiation skills • __________________ skills

KEY POINTS	EXAMPLES/EXPLANATIONS
⑩ ownership time	• = independence • ________ percent independent
⑪ student change	• consumer to ________________________________
⑫ teachers	• cannot ____________________ their work • they have ________________________________

After You Listen

D. Based on your notes, describe what you imagine the process of learning at the Khan Lab School would be like for one student for one hour. Write your notes on a separate page, and use five or more bullet points to show a sequence.

E. Indicate whether these statements are true or false, according to the video. If a statement is false, write the true one.

STATEMENTS	TRUE	FALSE
❶ Khan Lab School is also known as the Khan Academy. ________________________________	☐	☐
❷ Khan Lab School is looking for ways to reimagine education. ________________________________	☐	☐
❸ Self-paced refers to deciding how long you will spend on a topic. ________________________________	☐	☐
❹ Not being directed by an adult means other than a student's teachers. ________________________________	☐	☐
❺ Students need to learn by themselves at the second school because formal learning is not available. ________________________________	☐	☐
❻ Avoiding isolated students means ensuring that they have some social time. ________________________________	☐	☐
❼ Ownership time refers to parts of the day spent in teamwork. ________________________________	☐	☐
❽ Teachers cannot personalize their work because they have demands on their time. ________________________________	☐	☐

MyBookshelf > My eLab > Exercises > Chapter 7 > New Models for Education

F. Would you have wanted to attend elementary or secondary school that followed the models presented in Listening 2? Why or why not? Discuss in a group.

WARM-UP ASSIGNMENT

Give a Process Presentation

How do you do yoga? How was the first rocket invented? You often have to explain how to do something or how something was done in the past. These are examples of *processes*. Listening 1 talked about the process of adapting gaming principles to teaching different subjects. Listening 2 talked about schools challenging traditional ways of teaching. In this Warm-Up Assignment, you will outline a process you used to learn a new skill.

A. Choose a topic. Select something you learned that required several steps—for example, how to play a game, musical instrument, or sport, or a skill related to a job. Ask your teacher for approval of your topic.

B. Use this format and organize your presentation on a separate page. Refer to Focus on Critical Thinking (page 143) for suggestions on how to organize your ideas.

STEPS IN THE PROCESS	WHAT TO SAY
Introduce yourself and your topic.	Hello, my name is ________. Today, I'd like to explain the process of learning to ________.
Present the process in a logical order. Use transition words to signal the steps.	The process of learning to ________ involves ________ steps. The first step ... The next step ... Then, ... Finally, ...
Conclude with a summary. Explain where further information is available, and ask for questions.	In summary, learning to ________ is as easy as ________, ________, and ________. If you are interested in learning to ________, you can find more information (online/at the library/by talking to ...). Do you have any questions?

C. Practise your presentation with a partner. Use both body language (see Focus on Speaking, page 150). Make sure you use gerunds and infinitives correctly (see Focus on Grammar, page 148). Ask for feedback from your partner.

D. Present to the class. Ask your teacher and classmates for feedback on what could be improved. In the Final Assignment, your presentation or that of another student will form the basis of a seminar.

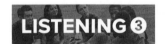

LISTENING 3

Three Approaches to Education

Education has been called "a history of untested hypotheses." This means that new ideas of how to teach and learn have been constantly introduced but not properly tested in a way that would show how one was superior to another. Many schools once trained students to enter factory-style jobs where they were simply expected to take orders. But the nature of work is shifting, and future jobs might be quite different when students graduate. In Listening 3, you will hear a lecture about three educational programs with different perspectives on what is important in education.

VOCABULARY BUILD

In the following exercises, explore key words from Listening 3.

A. Write short definitions for these words. Use a dictionary if needed.

1. **advocate:** ______________________________
2. **assumption:** ______________________________
3. **classic:** ______________________________
4. **liberal arts:** ______________________________

> Pronunciation: With new words, learn the difference between the stress on the verb "advocate" (long a) and the noun "advocate" (short a).

B. Fill in the blanks with the words that have the closest meaning to the words and phrases in bold.

appreciation	avalanche	ideology	sensitive

1. His **system of beliefs** (____________________) was based on relying on your own resources.
2. They wanted to express their **thanks** (____________________) to the school.
3. The teacher was **thoughtful and considerate** (____________________) about the student who could not read.
4. The **rocks that tumbled down** (____________________) blocked the highway.

C. These words will help you understand Listening 3. Fill in the blanks with the correct words to complete each sentence. Look up words you don't understand in a dictionary.

adversity	comradeship	nurturing
rhetoric	stamina	

1. The art of ____________________ includes techniques to help you argue, persuade, and motivate.
2. Sports help promote ____________________, or friendship among students.
3. Physical tasks that take ____________________ help build strength and character.
4. Teachers have a ____________________ role that lets them bring out the best in students.
5. We all face ____________________ in the form of challenges that must be overcome.

MyBookshelf > My eLab > Exercises > Chapter 7 > Vocabulary Review

D. VOCABULARY EXTENSION: The suffix *-ion* is often used to change verbs into nouns. For example, the key words *appreciation* and *assumption* come from the verb forms *appreciate* and *assume*. Write the verb forms of the following words from Listening 3. Discuss each one's meaning with a partner.

NOUN FORM	VERB FORM
1 application	
2 decision	
3 distraction	
4 education	
5 explanation	

NOUN FORM	VERB FORM
6 graduation	
7 innovation	
8 inspiration	
9 preparation	
10 solution	

Before You Listen

A. The composer John Cage (1912–1992) criticized college education as being about two hundred people reading the same book when two hundred people could read two hundred books. His point was that the traditional education system encourages everyone to think alike rather than giving them the chance to think differently and then compare individual ideas. If we followed Cage's advice, what might be some results from a college literature course with students reading two hundred different books?

____

____

____

B. Read this excerpt from Listening 3. Based on what is said, what do you think are the advantages and disadvantages of this approach to education? Discuss your answers with a partner.

> The first of the three schools I'd like to discuss is called the New Academy. It's a liberal arts college that aims to prepare learners for the future by exploring classic works of rhetoric, literature, and logic. This takes place in small seminars where students are encouraged to reflect, think, and debate the great issues of our time. All students at the New Academy learn Latin and Greek, as well as the social sciences: psychology, sociology, and law. It seems likely that a student from two hundred years ago would find the school quite familiar; its goal is to advocate—and build on—the best of what has worked in the past.

ADVANTAGES: ______________________________

____

DISADVANTAGES: ______________________________

____

While You Listen

C. Listening 3 is a lecture on three different educational programs. Read the categories in the table that will compare what the speaker has to say about each school. The first time you listen, try to get a general idea of how the schools differ. The second time you listen, fill in the details. Listen a third time to check your notes.

	THE NEW ACADEMY	FERN LAKE OUTDOOR EDUCATION CENTRE	COCOON
TYPE OF SCHOOL			computer futures centre
STRUCTURE			
PURPOSE			design a computer application
WHO THE STUDENTS ARE			
WHAT IS TAUGHT			
PHYSICAL EXERCISE			
WHAT THE STUDENTS DO AFTER			

After You Listen

D. Complete each of the following statements, according to the information in the listening. Then, discuss your answers with a partner.

1. By "nurturing the body as well as the mind," the speaker is suggesting ______________________________.

2. The mention of "team activities" is considered ______________________________.

3. When the speaker says "classrooms can seem so artificial," this probably means ______________________________.

4. The idea of letting students face adversity is ______________________________.

5. Facing problems and figuring out an approach is seen as ______________________________.

6. The phrase "prepare young people for the unknown" refers to ______________________________.

E. Based on the descriptions of the three programs, which would you most like to attend and why? Discuss your preferences in a group. Support your choice with what the speaker says about the program.

MyBookshelf > My eLab > Exercises > Chapter 7 > Three Approaches to Education

F. On a separate page, use your notes from Listening 3 to write a flow chart about the steps in the system of education used in one of the three schools. Base your flow chart on what you learned about process in Focus on Listening (page 142) and sequence in Focus on Critical Thinking (page 143). After, explain your flow chart to a partner.

Academic Survival Skill

Starting a Discussion with a Thesis Statement

When you have an academic discussion, as opposed to a casual conversation, you require a clear thesis, or point to be discussed. You also need evidence in the form of facts. Besides evidence, anecdotes, quotes, and rhetorical questions can help support your points.

A thesis statement usually promotes discussion by comparing two things, favouring one over the other. For example:

Online dictionaries offer more than paper dictionaries.

The thesis statement must have a clear point of view and be easy to understand. It should avoid unnecessary information and have a single argument, not a mix of two or more arguments.

A. Rewrite these thesis statements to make them clearer. Then, practise saying the statements with a partner.

1. Education systems—that is, different kinds of school systems used over the course of history—have mostly been about teaching, that is, the focus has been on the teacher, not the learner, and this is wrong.

   ____

   ____

2. When students are not doing their best, they should take responsibility for their work, and their attendance should be consistently good to be respectful to the teacher and other students.

   ____

   ____

3. Computers have many benefits and are also used to commit plagiarism and spread viruses.

   ____

   ____

Once you have a thesis, an academic discussion needs evidence. Imagine your thesis is:

As is common in a mastery-learning model, students should be able to retake exams until they achieve a perfect mark.

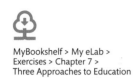

B. Which two of these three pieces of evidence would you use? Why? Discuss with a partner.

- ☐ When compared with students in traditionally taught classes, students in well-implemented mastery-learning classes consistently reach higher levels of achievement and develop greater confidence in their ability to learn and in themselves as learners.
- ☐ Mastery learning is an instructional strategy that results in a comprehensive grasp of curriculum as demonstrated through performance-based evaluations. Teachers support student mastery of material by providing guidance and assistance.
- ☐ Mastery-based learning was first introduced in the 1920s through the Winnetka Plan, an educational experiment engineered by district superintendent Carleton Washburne of Winnetka, Illinois. The experiment was inspired by John Dewey's (1859–1952) research in the University of Chicago Laboratory School.

Beyond evidence, discussions often include anecdotes (short personal stories that illustrate an idea), quotations (a famous person's words that distil wisdom on the topic), and rhetorical questions, which make people think.

C. In a group, discuss the following anecdote, quotation, and rhetorical question. How would each help support points in a discussion on mastery learning?

ANECDOTE:	I failed to get my driver's licence three times. Each time I failed for a different reason. By the time I got it, I knew I wouldn't make those same mistakes again.
QUOTATION:	Author Bram Stoker (1847–1912) said, "We learn from failure, not from success."
RHETORICAL QUESTION:	If we let student doctors retake their medical exams as often as they like, is it any guarantee they will remember the information after they graduate?

FINAL ASSIGNMENT

Explain a Process in a Seminar

Use what you learned in this chapter to take part in a seminar about improving a learning process.

A. Form a group of six. Choose one member's topic from the Warm-Up Assignment. Write a thesis statement for discussion. Use what you learned in Academic Survival Skill. For example, your thesis statement may be something like:

Teaching someone to ... could be improved by ... .

B. Ask your teacher to approve your topic and your thesis statement.

C. Prepare for your seminar individually. Collect evidence to support your view, as well as anecdotes and relevant quotations you can use to contribute to the discussion. Think of rhetorical questions you could ask.

D. Conduct your seminar in front of the class. When it is your turn to speak, use appropriate body language, hand gestures, and facial expressions (refer to Focus on Speaking, page 150). Vary your sentences with gerunds and infinitives (see Focus on Grammar, page 148).

E. During your seminar, listen carefully to what group members say, and look for opportunities to introduce your evidence, anecdotes, or quotations and to ask your rhetorical questions.

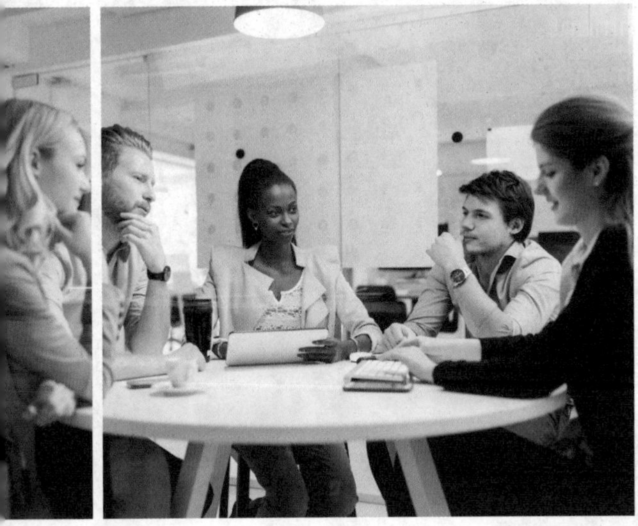

F. At the end, have one group member restate the thesis and briefly summarize the discussion.

G. As other groups present, take notes on a separate page answering these questions:

- What is the group's topic?
- Is the thesis statement clear?
- How well has the group addressed concerns in the thesis statement?
- Have the group members discussed the topic constructively, building on what each member said?
- Is the summary clear? Does it reflect what was discussed?

H. After all the groups have finished, share feedback on each group's performance.

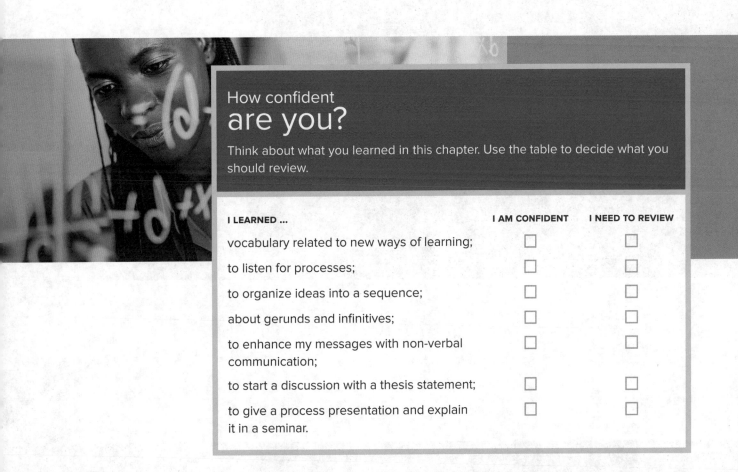

How confident are you?

Think about what you learned in this chapter. Use the table to decide what you should review.

I LEARNED ...	I AM CONFIDENT	I NEED TO REVIEW
vocabulary related to new ways of learning;	☐	☐
to listen for processes;	☐	☐
to organize ideas into a sequence;	☐	☐
about gerunds and infinitives;	☐	☐
to enhance my messages with non-verbal communication;	☐	☐
to start a discussion with a thesis statement;	☐	☐
to give a process presentation and explain it in a seminar.	☐	☐

CHAPTER 8

Finding Justice

A 1754 BCE carving of the Code of Hammurabi is among the oldest intact set of laws. It includes the infamous punishment "an eye for an eye." Although many of the Code's punishments were brutal and have long since been abandoned, aspects of the code, such as a right to a fair trial, are part of today's Universal Rights. Today's legal system is also faced with countless issues that Hammurabi could not have imagined: white-collar (business) crimes, computer-based crimes, and questions of when identity tracking becomes an illegal intrusion on a person's privacy.

How should society deal with old and new crimes in the twenty-first century?

In this chapter, you will

- learn vocabulary related to law and justice;
- distinguish fact from opinion;
- ask follow-up questions;
- review modals that express possibility;
- learn to construct an argument;
- use debate strategies;
- participate in a debate.

GEARING UP

A. Look at the image and then answer the questions.

1. Often found in front of courthouses, the statue of Lady Justice is rich in symbolism. What might the blindfold mean?

2. What might the balance scales symbolize?

3. What might be the meaning of the sword?

4. What might standing on a snake represent?

B. Discuss the questions and your answers, first with a partner, then in a group.

VOCABULARY BUILD OVERVIEW

Below are the key words you will practise in this chapter. Check the words you understand, then underline the words you use. Highlight the words you need to learn.

law and justice

nouns
databases*, dignity, estate sale*, genocide, indivisibility, infiltration, invasion, liability, mug shot, notion*, persecution, precedents*, self-determination, surveillance*

verbs
compiled*, conducting*, constrained*, expose*, indicate*, refined*, restore*, violate*

adverbs
collectively

adjectives
civil*, contemporary*, indispensable, inherited, innate, prejudiced

* Appears on the Academic Word List

FOCUS ON LISTENING

Distinguishing Fact from Opinion

When you listen to a speaker, you may wonder whether you are hearing facts or opinions. *Facts* are statements that are generally agreed to be true because they have been investigated or established by research and experiments. Sometimes facts are accepted after logically considering available evidence. For example, no one has been to another star system, but we can use observation, measurement, and logic to understand that stars exist.

Opinions are statements that reflect what someone thinks or feels about something. For example, if someone thinks humans will never travel to another star system, that is an opinion. However, there are also valid opinions. *Valid opinions* are opinions backed by evidence. For example, if someone explains that, even using the fastest of rockets, it would still take hundreds of years of travel to reach another star system and says, "It's unlikely anyone will visit another star system in the next five hundred years," then that's a *valid* opinion. You cannot argue about facts, but you can argue about opinions.

A. Read the comparisons of facts and opinions and the examples of valid opinions. Then, add other examples where needed.

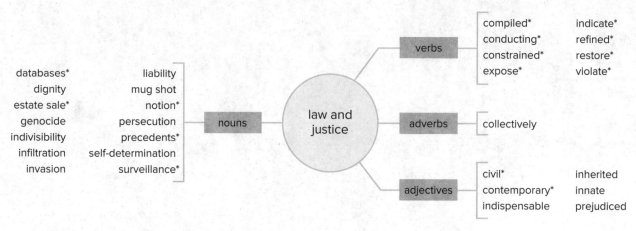

QUESTIONS	FACTS	OPINIONS	EXAMPLES OF VALID OPINIONS
IS IT TRUE?	Facts are scientifically proven or agreed upon by experts. Example: ____________ ____________ ____________	Opinions are personal beliefs that may not be shared by others. Example: *Prisons don't discourage criminals.* ____________	Prisons don't discourage criminals, as seen by the 41 to 44 percent of prisoners who reoffend within two years.

QUESTIONS	FACTS	OPINIONS	EXAMPLES OF VALID OPINIONS
DOES IT EXIST?	Facts can be observed first-hand by anyone. Example: *The Peel County Jail is now a museum.* ________________	Opinions cannot be observed or supported by proof. Example: ________________ ________________ ________________	Lots of people think jails are overcrowded because they believe the news reports.
HAS IT OCCURRED?	Even if something cannot be observed today, facts can be established by logical thought. Example: ________________ ________________ ________________	Opinions lack evidence or scientific credibility. Example: *Ancient Greek soldiers had to fight monsters.* ________________	Most ancient Greeks probably believed in monsters, based on ________________ ________________ ________________

B. Indicate whether each of these statements is fact, opinion, or valid opinion. Discuss your answers with a partner.

1. The legal system is far too easy on criminals. ________________
2. The fifty-three local car robberies probably mean people are forgetting to lock their car doors. ________________
3. In 2017, the police-reported Crime Severity Index (CSI) increased 2 percent, while the crime rate increased 1 percent. ________________
4. Crime is increasing because of violent video games and movies. ________________
5. Shoplifting is a huge problem, costing retailers $50 billion last year. ________________

C. Comparative and superlative adjectives (better/best) may signal opinions, along with statements that feature phrases like “I think” or “people say.” Vague words like *some* and *a few* may also signal opinions. Numerical data—statistics and dates—often indicate facts. Read these statements and highlight the words or phrases that suggest each is an opinion.

1. I’ve heard that white-collar criminals don’t usually go to jail.
2. Other than hurting someone, identity theft is the easiest kind of crime.
3. The leader of a country can’t be sent to prison while in office, or so people say.
4. Going to jail is a lot better for some people because they get food and a bed.
5. Everyone knows that stealing from a bank is worse than stealing from a store.
6. The stupidest crime anyone can commit is stealing a car.

!

When you challenge someone’s opinions, first try to see what facts you both agree on.

FOCUS ON CRITICAL THINKING

Asking Follow-Up Questions

"Yes. No. Yes. No. Maybe." In any conversation, you would probably find this string of answers frustrating and, most likely, you would ask follow-up questions. Follow-up questions have a couple of purposes. First, they signal your interest in what speakers are saying, encouraging them to continue. Often these follow-up questions are phrased in expressions like "Really?" "Did you?" "You can?" Secondly, follow-up questions allow you to check your understanding with reduced-form questions or by paraphrasing what you've heard.

A. Reduced-form questions refer to ones that begin with *who*, *what*, *when*, *where*, *why*, *how*, and *which*. These are questions that can stand alone or with a few other words rather than as a full question. This is possible because both the speaker and listeners understand the context of the question. Consider each sentence and full follow-up question. Write a second reduced-form question.

1. Someone I know kicked in my door and stole my stuff.

   FULL QUESTION: Who kicked in your door and stole your stuff?

   REDUCED-FORM QUESTION: *Who?*

2. A few weeks later, the thief was caught, charged by police, and sentenced by the court to a period in jail.

   FULL QUESTION: How long of a period was he sentenced to jail?

   REDUCED-FORM QUESTION: ______________________

3. Restorative justice is a means of connecting victims and criminal offenders.

   FULL QUESTION: Why do we need a means of connecting victims and criminal offenders?

   REDUCED-FORM QUESTION: ______________________

4. Restorative justice can help give victims what they need to understand, heal, and move on.

   FULL QUESTION: How can restorative justice help give victims what they need to understand, heal, and move on?

   REDUCED-FORM QUESTION: ______________________

5. Well, the best way to think about restorative justice is in the ways in which it contrasts to what our criminal justice process offers.

   FULL QUESTION: Which are the ways that restorative justice contrasts to what our criminal justice process offers?

   REDUCED-FORM QUESTION: ______________________

6. Communities are marginalized, and those are the groups that are most affected by crime in our communities.

   FULL QUESTION: How are communities marginalized, and how are those the groups that are most affected by crime in our communities?

   REDUCED-FORM QUESTION: ______________________

B. Follow-up questions also work with paraphrases of what has been said followed by questions such as "Is that right?" "Is that what you meant?" and "Have I understood correctly?" Paraphrases with questions can make speakers aware of what they have or have not fully explained. With a partner, paraphrase each of the following statements in fewer words, and add a question to check comprehension.

1. In Estonia, they've accepted the idea of a national ID card, and you have one card that does everything.

   Everyone has an ID card. Is that right?

2. The creepiest thing is that, when Target realized they were upsetting people, they came up with a creative strategy.

   ____

3. Remember the woman who won the $50 million lottery prize but didn't come forward to claim it, until they found a video showing her buying it?

   ____

4. So, in other words, if they can find who bought the ticket, they can find who bought other things.

   ____

5. The Disney Corporation tracks you just like the NSA.

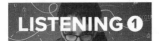

   ____

LISTENING 1

Technocreep

After looking up a recipe for pizza on the Internet, you suddenly find your other searches include pop-up advertisements for local Italian restaurants and flights to Italy. Everyone who has searched the Internet has had a similar experience, and it is one of the ways your privacy is being invaded by companies eager to sell goods and services. When do these kinds of activities cross the line and become illegal? In Listening 1, Tom Keenan talks about *technocreep*, the tendency for technology to creep (advance slowly) into our lives: stealing and using private information.

VOCABULARY BUILD

In the following exercises, explore key words from Listening 1.

A. Choose the phrase that best completes each sentence. Key words are in bold.

1. To investigate privacy issues, the university is **conducting** an experiment to see ________.
   a) how much private information people give away
   b) the number of public information workers
   c) how much public information people collect

2. It's important to **indicate** your choice when ________.
   a) you are told what to do
   b) there is no reason to act
   c) you vote in an election

3. In terms of **surveillance**, the government makes use of ________.
   a) a large staff to review tax returns
   b) cameras that can identify faces
   c) window blinds and soundproof rooms

4. The idea of **liability** relates to ________.
   a) insults spoken in courtrooms
   b) how often someone breaks the law
   c) the responsibility someone has

5. An **infiltration** of the membership of gangs ________.
   a) is one way police collect data
   b) relates to how gangs become police officers
   c) is one way in which groups can grow

B. Draw an arrow (↓) to indicate where in each sentence the word or phrase in parentheses should be placed.

1. (**3D imaging**) The process of the heart helped identify where to operate .
2. (**estate sale**) After the actor's death, an was held to sell his belongings .
3. (**invasion**) The of a country presents many opportunities for crime .
4. (**mug shot**) The police used a to match the criminal to the video .
5. (**databases**) When a crime has been committed, it is entered into one of the .

C. These words and phrases will help you understand Listening 1. Match each to its definition.

WORDS/PHRASES		DEFINITIONS
1 adjunct professor	_____	a) overspent on
2 capitalization	_____	b) country's system of identifying citizens
3 dovetail	_____	c) people pretending to be those who use violence politically
4 maxed out	_____	d) part-time professor
5 national ID	_____	e) radio frequency identification
6 NSA	_____	f) finding a way to create money from something
7 pseudo-terrorists	_____	g) fit together with
8 RFID	_____	h) National Security Agency

Before You Listen

A. Many high-technology devices now use scans of fingerprints, palms, faces, or irises (parts of your eye) for identification. When these are tied to your personal information, you become easy to track. What might be the dangers of sharing this kind of information? Discuss with a partner.

B. In this humorous excerpt from Listening 1, Mary takes a telephone order for a pizza from Mr. Kelly. Practise it with a partner and then discuss how it relates to concerns about privacy.

MARY: Is this Mr. Kelly? I show your national identification number as 6102049998-45-54610; is that correct?

MR. KELLY: Uh, yes. I'd like to order a couple of your double-meat special pizzas.

MARY: There will be a new twenty-dollar charge for this, sir.

MR. KELLY: What do you mean?

MARY: Sir, the system shows me that your medical records indicate that you have high blood pressure and extremely high cholesterol. Luckily, we have a new agreement with your national health-care provider that allows us to sell you double-meat pies as long as you agree to wave all future claims of liability.

MR. KELLY: What?

MARY: Gotta watch that waist if you're hitting the beach, eh? Forty-two inches, wow. Whoa, looks like you maxed out on all your credit cards. Bring cash, okay?

While You Listen

C. Before you listen, read the interview questions. The first time you listen, try to understand the gist. Listen a second time to fill in the answers and a third time to check and add details, noting which information is opinion or fact. Ask yourself whether or not you agree with Keenan's opinions.

INTERVIEW QUESTIONS	RESPONSES AND ARGUMENT
❶ Listening to that pizza ad, the call-in there, how far-fetched is that?	*It's real. (fact)* *The national ID number is used for all services in Estonia, but North America pushes back. (fact)* *Target/pregnant girl example (fact)*
❷ Wow, they tracked buying habits. How did they do that?	
❸ So, how do you define *technocreep*?	
❹ So, we have heard for some time that technology is compromising our privacy. You say that we're actually in a new era of infiltration?	
❺ So, in other words, if they can find who bought the ticket, they can find who bought other things. They can actually link you up to lots of other things?	
❻ What precisely are they doing?	
❼ The American government is conducting an experiment right now called BOSS: Biometric Optical Surveillance System. Does that somehow dovetail with what you're talking about?	
❽ So you're saying that potential for misuse is great, but who's going to do the misusing?	

After You Listen

D. Answer the following questions to better understand Keenan's arguments against technocreep.

1. Why are stores anxious to assign a personal identification number to individual customers?

____

____

2. What was the Target department store's reaction after being criticized for predicting a girl was pregnant and sending her pregnancy-related advertisements?

____

____

____

3. Why does Keenan find it disturbing to shop for a chandelier, and then see Google advertisements for other chandeliers pop up?

____

____

____

4. Why is it a concern that a woman who bought a winning lottery ticket was tracked by video?

____

____

____

5. How does the Calgary Police Service use its facial recognition system?

____

____

____

6. How might videotaping people outside polling stations be used against them?

____

____

____

7. Although the use of a BOSS system is meant to identify terrorists in a crowd, how could it be abused?

____

____

____

8. Why are Disney theme parks eager to have each visitor wear a bracelet with an identifying chip?

____

____

____

Develop Your Vocabulary: "Technocreep" is a made-up compound word. A speaker using such a word will likely define it. If not, ask.

MyBookshelf > My eLab > Exercises > Chapter 8 > Technocreep

E. The focus of this chapter is law and justice. New laws are created when people believe they are being treated unjustly. Based on Listening 1, choose the statement that suggests the best reason that new laws around technocreep might be created.

- ☐ If we continue to let technology collect personal information, it is likely that a new form of computer will someday control us all.
- ☐ Personal information may be freely available or even given away, but it's hard to decide when sharing benefits you.
- ☐ Your private information is your personal property, and others using it without your permission are stealing.

FOCUS ON GRAMMAR

Modals That Express Possibility

As you listened to the interview in Listening 1, you heard the speakers using modal auxiliaries. *Modal auxiliaries* are sometimes called "helping verbs": they work with other verbs to express ideas about time and mood. Common modals include: *shall*, *could*, *must*, *ought to*, *should*, and *would*. One class of modals expresses possibility.

FUNCTIONS	MODAL	EXAMPLES	EXPLANATION
future actions, states, intentions, and high possibility	will	I **will** call the police officer *in five minutes*.	It is going to happen.
general possibility, ability	can	I **can** call a police officer *anytime I want*.	It is possible to do so.
weak possibility	might	I **might** call a police officer *if I am worried*.	It is not certain you will do so, but it is a possibility.
weaker possibility or permission	may	I **may** call a police officer *if I think it is necessary*.	
weakest possibility	could	I **could** call a police officer *if there was a problem*.	

RULES	EXAMPLES
Use modals with the base form of the verb.	He **can run**. They **may run**.
Do not modify the main verb.	She **could hide**. We **will hide**.

A. Write questions using these words and modal auxiliaries.

1. will / twenty-dollar / charge

____

2. might / see / now / friends

____

3. can / computer's / privacy / help / settings

____

4. may / bank / someone / talk

____

5. could / confession / without / signed / convict

____

B. Write sentences on an aspect of technocreep issues around privacy. For each sentence, use a modal auxiliary that illustrates the following functions.

1. future actions, states, intentions, and high possibility: _______________

   ____

2. general possibility, ability: _______________

   ____

3. weak possibility: _______________

   ____

4. weaker possibility or permission: _______________

   ____

5. weakest possibility: _______________

   ____

! Use what you learned about modals when you prepare assignments.

MyBookshelf > My eLab > Exercises > Chapter 8 > Grammar Review

LISTENING 2 Debate: *Parallel Cases from under the Pear-Tree*

It is easy to forget that there are different legal systems with different views of law and justice. For example, some countries have laws that can send students to prison for cheating on exams. Ancient China had one of the earliest and longest-lasting legal systems, but, at that time, studying law was not considered a noble pursuit. For this reason, a new magistrate (a position that combined detective, prosecutor, and judge) relied on books describing cases to help learn the profession. Listening 2 is a debate on the magistrate system, asking whether or not that system could work today.

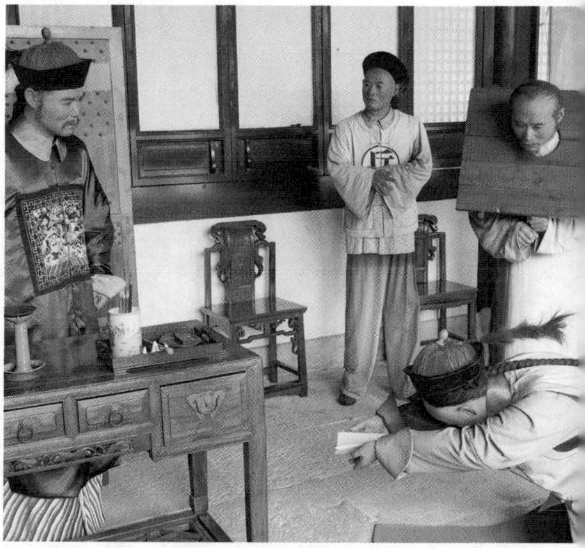

VOCABULARY BUILD

In the following exercises, explore key words from Listening 2.

A. Fill in the blanks with the correct words to complete the paragraph.

civil	expose	prejudiced	refined	restore

Judges are part of the ____________________ service and follow its rules. They cannot be ____________________ against any criminal. Some judges would like to ____________________ old punishments, particularly the death penalty. However, opponents are quick to ____________________ the unfairness of such a punishment, such as the many innocent people falsely accused of murder. Laws have been ____________________ over centuries in order to preserve innocent people's freedom.

B. Match each word to its definition.

WORDS		DEFINITIONS
1 precedents	______	a) restricted in some way
2 constrained	______	b) received property, sometimes after the death of a relative
3 compiled	______	c) belonging to the present time
4 contemporary	______	d) previous legal rulings that are considered during trials
5 inherited	______	e) put together

C. VOCABULARY EXTENSION: Choose the word from task A that can be used to complete all of the following sentences.

1. Rudeness was not allowed and everyone was warned to be ____________________.
2. His work as a ____________________ engineer involved the construction of roads and bridges.
3. The idea of a ____________________ society is to consider individuals before government and business.
4. A ____________________ war is when a country divides into two parties that fight.
5. We chained ourselves to the courthouse gates as an act of ____________________ disobedience.

6 Refusing to treat them equally was a violation of their ________________ rights.

D. These words and phrases will help you understand Listening 2. Fill in the blanks with the correct words to complete the paragraph.

adversarial	community service	impartially	innocence
judgments	prosecution	recants	testimony

The Western justice system is based on a/an ________________ model in which one side, the ________________, tries to show a person's guilt, while the other side, the defence, tries to demonstrate ________________. During a trial, ________________ is heard from witnesses before a judge ________________ gives a verdict, or decision. These ________________ can include fines, prison, or ________________—for example, asking a graffiti artist to clean up others' graffiti. The legal system doesn't always work, such as when an innocent person is sent to prison until new evidence is found or a witness ________________—that is, admits earlier testimony was false.

The prosecution acts on behalf of the government.

Before You Listen

A. A debate involves two people or two groups arguing either side of a proposition —a debatable statement. After one person presents several points, it's the duty of the other side to rebut—or reject—the points, using logical arguments as well as passionate opinions. In the end, a judge or an audience decides whose arguments have prevailed (won) and whose have failed. With a partner, think of and discuss points for and against this proposition about restoring the ancient Chinese magistrate position.

THE PROPOSITION: The modern judge, prosecutor, and detective should be one person.

B. The following is an example of a traditional magistrate's creative solution to a problem. Why would such a solution be unlikely today? Discuss with a partner.

Modern judges are mostly constrained to giving out punishments in terms of jail time, fines, and community service. There is little creativity. Compare this to Chang Ch'i-hsien's solution to the problem of two heirs, each of whom complained about the division of their inherited property, claiming the other's property was better. Chang simply forced each to move to the other's house and land.

While You Listen

C. The first time you listen, try to understand the debate arguments put forth by each side. Listen a second time and take notes. Focus on the arguments and ignore the examples. Listen a third time and decide which of the arguments are based on fact and which are based on opinion.

FOR THE PROPOSITION	AGAINST THE PROPOSITION
1 • Judges favour law over justice. (opinion) • ____________________ ____________________	• Judges don't favour law over justice. (opinion) • ____________________ ____________________
2 • Combining the roles of judge ____________ ____________________ ____________________	• ____________________ • ____________________ ____________________
3 • Magistrates would be ____________ ____________________ ____________________	• ____________________ • ____________________ ____________________
4	• Magistrate position ____________ ____________________
5	• It takes many years ____________ ____________________
6 • ____________________ ____________________ ____________________	• The magistrate system was open to abuse. (valid opinion) • ____________________ ____________________
7 • No one could be convicted without a signed confession, ____________	• ____________________ ____________________
8 • Magistrates motivated: ____________ ____________________ ____________________	• ____________________ ____________________ ____________________
9 • A magistrate's wisdom ____________ ____________________ ____________________	• ____________________ ____________________ ____________________

After You Listen

D. Choose the phrase that best completes each sentence.

1. When they began their careers, Chinese magistrates ________.
   a) were already well trained
   b) had usually written a book of cases
   c) were generally unprepared

2. The case of the woman driving her car on the sidewalk is meant to show ________.
   a) a judge's creativity in giving out punishment
   b) the foolishness of people around school buses
   c) how unfair driving laws are still widely practised

3. The case of a criminal writing on top of a contract's ink stamp ________.
   a) shows the rich traditions of the Chinese magistrates
   b) points out an example of an unfit magistrate
   c) indicates the difficult crimes magistrates had to solve

4. In the case of the boat builders, the magistrate burned the boat ________.
   a) as a warning against using expensive materials
   b) as punishment for safety issues
   c) in order to count the nails being used

5. The case of the widow and the two pigs is used to explain ________.
   a) how Chinese magistrates were skilled detectives
   b) the proper ceremonies used to honour the dead
   c) how a smell led to a woman being charged with murder

Many discussions are informal debates and work best when facts, not opinions or emotions, are used to make decisions.

MyBookshelf > My eLab > Exercises > Chapter 8 > Debate: *Parallel Cases*

E. Listening 2 ends before the two sides have an opportunity to summarize their findings. Pick one side and use your notes to write a brief summary, on a separate page, supporting your chosen side's arguments. Share your summary with a partner who has summarized the other side.

FOCUS ON SPEAKING

Constructing an Argument

Think of the last time you argued for something. In Chapter 7 (Academic Survival Skill page 159), you learned how to construct a thesis and give evidence to support your thesis. Once you have a thesis statement, you also need an approach—a structure for presenting your thesis and argument. An *argument* is a way of organizing ideas to guide others to a conclusion. Constructing an argument also requires understanding your audience and taking into account the time you have to speak and the venue where you will be presenting.

A. Once you have your thesis and evidence, construct your argument. Match these steps for constructing an argument to the explanations.

STEPS		EXPLANATIONS
❶ PROVIDE A CONTEXT	______	a) In a longer argument, briefly explain the points that you are going to discuss. In a shorter argument, simply say: *There are three points/ reasons/arguments. The first one is ...* Avoid casual language, contractions, and slang. Define technical terms: *Incarceration, or imprisonment/confinement, means ...*
❷ GIVE AN OVERVIEW	______	b) After you finish, invite the audience to ask about anything they did not understand. Use your answers to emphasize parts of your argument.
❸ EXPLAIN THE THESIS STATEMENT	______	c) Use the evidence that is most likely to capture the audience's attention. Don't wait to share your best examples and ideas.
❹ START WITH A PROMINENT EXAMPLE	______	d) Explain what your thesis statement means. Most arguments are about making a change, so you may want to talk about why the current situation is unacceptable.
❺ USE SIGNPOSTING	______	e) Keep track of time and, just before you are done, restate your main points and thesis. Finish by asking the audience to change their minds or take some action.
❻ CONCLUDE WITH A SUMMARY AND ASK FOR CHANGE	______	f) Use numbers and other expressions to let your audience know where you are in your speech: *First, ..., My second point ..., Finally, ... To summarize, ... In conclusion, ...*
❼ ASK FOR QUESTIONS	______	g) Relate the topic to your audience or yourself: *Today's topic relates to the tragic events that happened in our community last month ...* or *As someone whose aunt was a judge/prison guard/police officer, I know about ...*

B. Using the topic of graffiti, work with a partner and take turns practising a brief presentation for the proposition: Writing graffiti is an offence that needs to be taken more seriously. Use the steps in task A to structure your argument.

STEPS	PRESENTATION EXAMPLE
❶ PROVIDE A CONTEXT	When I was walking here today, I passed several walls that had been covered with racist graffiti. I would like to explain how graffiti impacts victims and why graffiti offenders should be made aware of it.
❷ GIVE AN OVERVIEW	I'd like to explain the problem of graffiti with three points.
❸ EXPLAIN THE THESIS STATEMENT	Understanding graffiti requires distinguishing amoung the three main kinds: so-called art, tagging (signing), and gang-related tags that mark out territory.
❹ START WITH A PROMINENT EXAMPLE	In 2019, it was estimated that 10 percent of American graffiti was gang-related. This means ...
❺ USE SIGNPOSTING	First, gang graffiti makes younger kids think being in a gang is cool. Second, ...
❻ CONCLUDE WITH A SUMMARY AND ASK FOR CHANGE	I've explained how graffiti has financial impacts: impacts on gang membership and impacts on community feelings of safety. But those who write graffiti are only given fines and sentences. It's time for more serious consequences, for offenders to face their victims, and ...
❼ ASK FOR QUESTIONS	Now, I would be happy to take any questions.

MyBookshelf > My eLab > Exercises > Chapter 8 > Focus on Speaking

WARM-UP ASSIGNMENT

Construct an Argument for a Debate

In Focus on Speaking, you learned how to construct an argument and share it in a presentation. Now construct an argument for a debate that will be held in the Final Assignment. You can choose to argue either for or against the following proposition:

In a legal system, human rights are more important than laws.

A. Use the format you learned in Focus on Speaking to organize your argument.

STEPS	NOTES
❶ PROVIDE A CONTEXT	
❷ GIVE AN OVERVIEW	
❸ EXPLAIN THE THESIS STATEMENT	
❹ START WITH A PROMINENT EXAMPLE	
❺ USE SIGNPOSTING	
❻ CONCLUDE WITH A SUMMARY AND ASK FOR CHANGE	
❼ ASK FOR QUESTIONS	

!

Pronunciation: When you speak to a group, you might talk faster, slurring words together and making them difficult to understand. Take breaths and slow down.

B. Discuss your argument with a partner. Refer to Focus on Grammar (page 172) as you discuss possibilities.

C. Ask for feedback from your teacher and partner to see what you could improve. Save your argument for the Final Assignment.

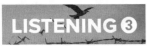

LISTENING 3

VIDEO

Human Rights

The history of human rights has been a centuries-long march to give everyone the same rights as are enjoyed by the wealthy and powerful. Women and ethnic groups have had to fight for rights to be educated, vote, own property, and make their own life decisions, such as whom they might marry. But these rights, once gained, are not eternal; no matter what rights have been made legal, cruel governments can quickly overturn them. It's important for everyone to stand up for their own human rights and those of others.

VOCABULARY BUILD

In the following exercises, explore key words from Listening 3.

A. Highlight the word or phrase in parentheses that best completes each sentence. Key words are in bold.

1. They were **collectively** held responsible; (none / some) of them escaped justice.
2. A person's **dignity** is something that helps them (embrace / resist) insults.
3. His talent was **innate**, meaning it was (developing / within him).
4. His **notion** was a new (skin cream / idea).
5. In terms of **self-determination**, she had a right not to be (a slave / employed).

B. Choose the best definition for each word in bold. Use a dictionary to check your answers.

1	**genocide**	a) a genetic experiment	b) killing an ethnic group
2	**indispensable**	a) not exactly necessary	b) absolutely necessary
3	**indivisibility**	a) unable to be divided	b) able to be divided
4	**persecution**	a) harassment	b) sue in court
5	**violate**	a) form an agreement	b) break an agreement

C. Knowing the following words will help you better understand Listening 3. Use the context of each word in bold to write a definition.

1. Human rights apply to every person in every part of the world, without exception. They are therefore **universal**.

   ____

2. The first dimension: the classic political and civil liberty rights. These include the right to life and physical **integrity**.

   ____

3. The right to the highest **attainable** standard of physical and mental health.

   ____

4. Human rights can only be **consummated** when all facets work together.

___

5. And who exactly has the job of **implementing** and upholding human rights?

___

6. For example, it works to end the **recruitment** of child soldiers.

___

7. But a crucial step has been taken: war criminals can no longer commit their **transgressions** with impunity.

___

8. Are there any controversial aspects about Human Rights as well? Yes, there are two main points of **contention**.

___

MyBookshelf > My eLab > Exercises > Chapter 8 > Vocabulary Review

Before You Listen

A. What human rights do you have? With a partner, list five and then rank them from most (1) to least (5) important. Then compare your list and rankings in a group.

___

___

___

___

___

B. Read a paragraph from Listening 3 and highlight the opinions. Are the opinions valid or not? Discuss the reasons for your choice with a partner.

> "All human beings are born free and equal in dignity and rights." This is what it says in the very first Article of the Universal Declaration of Human Rights of 10 December 1948. The notion of human rights has become one of the most important in the history of humankind.

While You Listen

C. The first time you watch, complete the statements. Then watch again and decide which of the speaker's statements are facts or opinions (including valid opinions). If you are unsure, refer to Focus on Listening (page 164).

STATEMENTS	FACT	OPINION
1 We describe human rights as those rights which apply ___	☐	☐
2 Human rights are part of international law. ___	☐	☐

STATEMENTS	FACT	OPINION
❸ These declarations are collectively known as the International Bill of Human Rights and are ____________	☐	☐
❹ Human rights are often divided into three ____________	☐	☐
❺ The exercise of civil and political rights depends on the safeguarding of ____________	☐	☐
❻ Countries carry the main responsibility ____________	☐	☐
❼ The UN's central body is the Human Rights Council, a body of ____________	☐	☐
❽ Civil society has an especially ____________	☐	☐
❾ Non-governmental organizations such as Amnesty International ____________ ____________	☐	☐
❿ The creation of independent national institutes for human rights, which have ____________	☐	☐
⓫ The notion of human rights originates in the West and ____________	☐	☐
⓬ Western countries are accused of using human rights as a pretext for military intervention ____________ ____________	☐	☐
⓭ Respect for and protection of human rights ____________ ____________	☐	☐

After You Listen

D. Read the following statements and indicate whether each is true or false, according to the text. Write the correct statement for those that are false.

STATEMENTS	TRUE	FALSE
1 Human Rights apply equally to everyone regardless of features that may distinguish one person from another.	☐	☐
2 A number of UN Conventions, such as the Convention on the Rights of the Child, are not related to human rights.	☐	☐
3 The principle of indivisibility means that all rights are separate.	☐	☐
4 The UN carries the main responsibility for safeguarding human rights.	☐	☐
5 All countries on the Council uphold human rights.	☐	☐
6 The International Criminal Court in The Hague investigates and passes sentence on genocide, war crimes, and crimes against humanity.	☐	☐
7 Non-governmental organizations monitor the observance of human rights in places all over the world.	☐	☐
8 Following the attacks of 9/11, measures were introduced that compromised human rights.	☐	☐

E. Answer these questions with a partner, and then discuss your answers in a group. As you discuss, use what you learned in Focus on Critical Thinking (page 166) to ask follow-up questions.

1. The first dimension of human rights is the classic political and civil liberty rights. Give two examples of these rights.

   ____

2. The second dimension of human rights is economic, social, and cultural human rights. Give two examples of these rights.

   ____

3. The third dimension deals with the rights of groups. Give two examples of these rights.

   ____

4. Some argue that human rights originate in the West and cannot simply be transferred to other cultures. What is an argument against this?

   ____

5 When some United Nations countries commit human rights abuses themselves, should they be removed from the United Nations? Think of one reason why they should, and one reason why they should not.

____

F. Consider the poem by Martin Niemöller (1892–1984), writing about those arrested by Nazis during World War II in Germany. What message do the words express, and how are they still relevant today? Compare your answers in a group.

First they came for the socialists, and I did not speak out—because I was not a socialist.

Then they came for the trade unionists, and I did not speak out—because I was not a trade unionist.

Then they came for the Jews, and I did not speak out—because I was not a Jew.

Then they came for me—and there was no one left to speak for me.

____

____

____

MyBookshelf > My eLab > Exercises > Chapter 8 > Human Rights

Academic Survival Skill

Using Debate Strategies

In Focus on Speaking (page 177), you learned how to construct an argument in a presentation. But winning an argument requires using strategies that will convince both your opponent and other listeners. You also need to identify weaknesses in others' arguments.

The most important thing in a debate is to remain polite. Being rude will not impress your opponent or the audience. Attack the arguments instead of attacking the character of those giving the arguments (e.g., suggesting they are foolish). Attacking a debater's character is so common, it has a name—*ad hominem*, which is Latin for *argument to the person*. Recognizing this and other common logical fallacies (thinking errors) is an easy way to dismiss your opponents' arguments. In this case, you can say: "My opponents may wish to attack me, but it is only because they are unable to attack my arguments."

! There are dozens of common logical fallacies. Look for others online.

A. Read the following logical fallacies and examples, and explain why each example argument might be false.

LOGICAL FALLACIES AND EXPLANATIONS	EXAMPLE ARGUMENTS
1 **Appeal to authority arguments** are based on the ideas of a respected person or source. Challenge the qualifications of the source to point out that the ideas are not current or applicable to the thesis.	Albert Einstein said that peace cannot be kept by force; it can only be kept by understanding. ____________ ____________
2 **Slippery slope arguments** suggest one thing will lead to more serious things. Challenge the basic assumptions and suggest the serious consequences are unrelated.	Shoplifting has to be treated seriously before offenders grow up to be murderers. ____________ ____________

LOGICAL FALLACIES AND EXPLANATIONS	EXAMPLE ARGUMENTS
❸ **False dichotomy arguments** suggest that there are only two choices. Challenge by pointing out that there are almost always other choices.	Either you get a job now or you'll be unemployed for the rest of your life. ____________ ____________
❹ **Ad populum arguments** suggest that the majority is always right. Challenge by pointing out examples of when the majority has been wrong.	Prison sentences are too short. At least 67 percent of people agree. ____________ ____________

FINAL ASSIGNMENT

Participate in a Debate

Use everything you learned in this chapter to participate in a debate related to laws and human rights.

A. Form a group of six. Choose as your topic for debate a criminal offence that has been committed. You can select one from a recent news story or an older crime. Each group will present their debate in front of the class.

B. Combine the crime you have identified with the arguments you developed for or against the proposition in the Warm-Up Assignment.

Human rights are more important than laws. For example, in cases of ____________.

C. Three group members will argue for the proposition, and three will argue against it. If you argued the opposite point of view in the Warm-Up Assignment, you can use your ideas to anticipate and counter the other side's arguments.

D. Do your research. Use the library and the Internet to find out more about the crime and human rights and laws that relate to it. Be sure to consider victim's rights, not just the rights of the criminal.

E. Plan your debate. Use this format to organize the debate and write your notes on separate pages. Construct your arguments based on what you learned in Focus on Speaking (page 177). Use modal auxiliaries to express possibility (see Focus on Grammar, page 172). Be prepared to use what you learned in Focus on Critical Thinking (page 166) to ask follow-up questions during the rebut stage of the debate.

IN FAVOUR OF THE PROPOSITION	AGAINST THE PROPOSITION
❶ State the proposition and define what it means. Present three points in favour.	❷ Rebut the other team's points; this may include their interpretation of the proposition. Present three points against.
❸ Rebut the other team's points and add new points.	❹ Rebut the other team's points and add new points.
❺ Summarize your points and objections to the other team's points, and explain why your team's points have helped the proposition prevail (i.e., succeed).	❻ Summarize your points and objections to the other team's points, and explain why your team's points have made the proposition fail.

F. Agree on the amount of time each of your team members has to speak.

G. Conduct your debate. As you participate, use what you learned in Focus on Listening (page 164) to separate opponents' facts from opinions and try to spot logical fallacies (see Academic Survival Skill, page 184).

H. After your debate, vote on which side had the more effective arguments—for or against the proposition. Once all groups have presented, ask your teacher and classmates for advice on how you might improve your presentation's content and style.

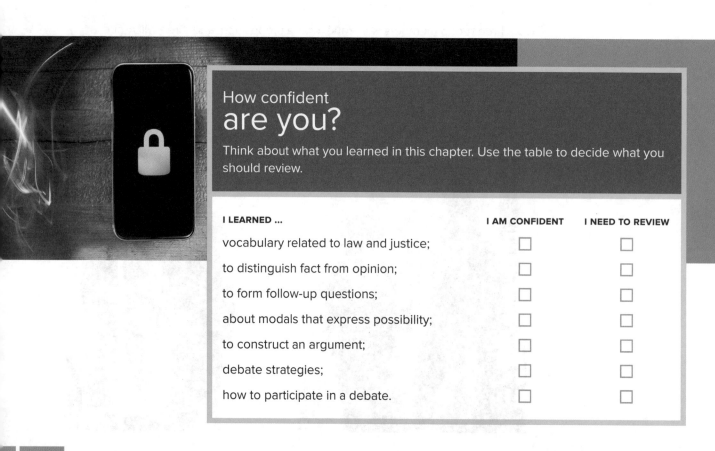

How confident are you?

Think about what you learned in this chapter. Use the table to decide what you should review.

I LEARNED ...	I AM CONFIDENT	I NEED TO REVIEW
vocabulary related to law and justice;	☐	☐
to distinguish fact from opinion;	☐	☐
to form follow-up questions;	☐	☐
about modals that express possibility;	☐	☐
to construct an argument;	☐	☐
debate strategies;	☐	☐
how to participate in a debate.	☐	☐

APPENDIX 1
Conversation Gambits

Gambits are ways of starting, maintaining, and closing informal and formal conversations in polite ways. Practise the following on your own and with a partner.

GAMBITS	INFORMAL	FORMAL
OFFER GREETINGS	Hi. How are you?	Hello. How are you?
INTRODUCE A TOPIC	I'd like to talk to you about ...	If you have a moment, I would like to discuss ...
EXPLAIN A POINT	Let me explain. Here's the idea. What do you think about ...?	Let me suggest ... The basic idea is ... The important part of the idea is ...
CHECK FOR COMPREHENSION	Do you get what I'm saying? Do you follow what I've said so far?	Can I ask if you understand my point? Is everything clear so far?
SHOW YOU ARE LISTENING	[frown, nod] Really? Right. Uh-huh. OK.	[frown, nod] Yes. Are you sure?
SHOW AGREEMENT	Yes. I agree. I can't argue with that.	Yes. I agree. That's true. You've made a good point.
INTERRUPT	I'm sorry, ... Excuse me, ... Pardon me, but ... Can I ask a question? Can I add something here?	Sorry for interrupting, but ... If I can just interrupt for a moment, ... If I could stop you there for a second, ...
ASK THE SPEAKER TO REPEAT	Can you say that again? Could you repeat that? What was that? Excuse me? Sorry, what?	I'm not sure I follow. Would you mind repeating that? Pardon me, what did you say?
REFUSE INTERRUPTIONS	Please, let me finish. Can I just finish my point?	Perhaps if you could let me finish. May I just finish my point?
CONTINUE AFTER AN INTERRUPTION	As I was saying, ... Let's see, where was I?	To get back to what I was saying, ...
DISAGREE POLITELY	That's not true/right, is it? I'd say/think something different ...	I'm not sure I agree. I can't say that that's a convincing point/argument.
MAKE A QUALIFICATION	That's not exactly what I meant.	Although I agree with ..., I also believe ...
EXPRESS AN OPINION	In my opinion, ... What I think ... As I see it, ...	My personal opinion is that ...
CLARIFY THE SPEAKER'S POINTS BY RESTATING	So, what you mean is ... So, what you're trying to say is ...	If I can restate, I understand your point is ...
CLARIFY YOUR POINTS BY RESTATING	What I'm trying to say is ... What I mean is ...	To put it another way, ... Let me explain it another way ...
SUMMARIZE	All in all, what I'm saying is ... The main points are ...	To summarize, ... To bring this all together, ...
CLOSE THE CONVERSATION	I have to go now, but it's been great talking with you. Thanks for the chance to talk.	I'm glad we had a chance to talk. Thank you for taking the time to speak with me.

APPENDIX 2
Strategies for Improving Listening and Speaking Skills

1. Listening is made up of understanding the sounds and meanings of words as well as the pronunciation patterns of words, phrases, and sentences. **In your spare time, take the opportunity to listen to podcasts in your field of study as well as recordings of short stories and novels.** Listen several times, first to get the gist and the general patterns of pronunciation, then to understand new vocabulary in context. While you listen, try pronouncing portions of what you are hearing.

2. When you listen, you acquire new vocabulary, new ideas, and new ways of saying things. Research shows that simply listening to a lecture will lead to limited acquisition. Instead, you need to activate what you have heard by taking notes, reviewing them, and trying to use the language in other contexts, such as in a discussion with a study partner. The most effective way of learning new ideas is to teach. **Take what you've heard in a lecture, organize it, and share it with another person.** In this way, you are more likely to remember new words, expressions, and ideas.

3. **Whenever you listen, remind yourself of your purpose.** In some cases, you may listen passively, not bothering to remember most of the information you hear. For example, if you are in an airport, you will hear hundreds of announcements but only need to worry about those related to your flight. In other cases, you need to listen actively, measuring each idea you hear in terms of what it means to you. You might listen to understand, to summarize, to make a decision, or for other purposes. Knowing the purpose helps you focus on what to listen for.

4. **Interrupting is a key part of listening.** When you are in a conversation, one of the simplest and most basic ways to interrupt is to appear confused or frown. The other speaker will often take this as a cue to pause and explain in greater detail. Otherwise, stop the other speaker and politely ask for clarification. The speaker may repeat what was said, paraphrase the idea, provide an explanation, or provide an example. If the clarification satisfies you, smile and nod. If not, ask questions to help you better understand.

5. **Listening strategies include top down and bottom up approaches.** In a *top down* approach, you listen to predict what the talk will be about (based on your background knowledge), to identify the main idea, to draw inferences (guesses based on the facts), and to summarize ideas. In a *bottom up* approach, you tend to listen for specific information, such as key words, directions, or instructions. In bottom up listening, the main idea is not as important and you can't necessarily summarize the ideas effectively. Understanding why you are listening helps you choose between top down and bottom up approaches.

6. When you speak, you often end up repeating certain questions, answers, and statements. For example, you may ask questions when you meet someone new, provide answers about yourself, and make statements about everything from the weather to the latest news. For both informal and formal situations, practise these conversations in your head and say them out loud, adding details that help make you seem friendlier. **Find opportunities to speak.** For example, try engaging in short conversations with other commuters or people where you study or work.

7. You might not speak as much as you would like to because you become nervous in classroom conversations or social situations where you have to speak in front of a group of people. In these situations, you might feel that you cannot express yourself properly, perhaps because you cannot grasp the right words or keep up with what others are saying. But it's better to try and sometimes fail than to avoid speaking more than necessary. **Practising speaking is the principal way to improve your speaking skills.**

8. **In academic situations where you need to make a presentation in front of a class, spend as much time as possible on preparation, rehearsing what you have to say until it feels conversational.** Don't memorize it but speak as though you are explaining the ideas in a relaxed way to a close friend for the first time. Use confident body language and maintain eye contact with at least three people: one on either side of the room and one in the middle. This gives the impression that you're looking at everyone. Smile; smiling will help to relax both you and your audience.

9. **During classes and lectures, ask permission to record part of what you hear on your mobile phone or other audio device.** After class, listen to portions and improve your speaking skills by taking time to repeat what you have heard several times. This helps you with intonation patterns and the pronunciation of key words and expressions related to the speaker's ideas. This not only prepares you to discuss the ideas in class, but also serves as an effective study aid.

10. **When you are tested on speaking, it is often done as an interview in which you must also understand the questions you hear.** The most important thing is to ensure that you understand the question or speaking prompt. If you are not sure, politely ask for clarification. Take a moment to consider your answer and then focus on giving a complete answer. Don't try to say as little as possible to avoid making mistakes. If, part way through your answer you realize you have misunderstood the question, ask for the chance to begin again. This is better than delivering an incomplete or wrong answer.

To really improve your English, take every opportunity to read, write, speak, and listen.

PHOTO CREDITS

GETTY IMAGES

pp. viii, 92, 93 (background), 115 (bottom): © Marco Vacca; pp. ix, 116, 117 (background), 139 (bottom): © peepo; pp. ix, 140, 141 (background), 161 (bottom): © Pekic; pp. ix, 162, 163 (background), 186: © Westend61.

NASA

pp. iv, viii, 68, 69 (background), 91 (bottom): © NASA.

SHUTTERSTOCK

pp. iv, 5: © alphaspirit; pp. iv, 29: © Ezume Images; pp. iv, 69 (middle): © Macrovector; pp. iv, 70: © Goodluz; pp. v, 61: © tomasekas01; pp. v, 66: © Daxiao Productions; pp. v, 67 (bottom): © Atstock Productions; pp. v, 150: © PathDoc; pp. viii, 2–3, 23 (bottom): © Sergey Tinyakov; pp. viii, 24–25, 43 (bottom): © Robert Kneschke; pp. 4: © BigTunaOnline; p. 7: © Andrey_Popov; p. 9: © Matej Kastelic; p. 10: © Rawpixel.com; p. 12: © Rawpixel.com; p. 15: © Georgios Kollidas; p. 17: © Luis Molinero; p. 19: © Hyejin Kang; p. 20: © Monkey Business Images; p. 23 (top): © Muh; p. 26: © HappyAprilBoy; p. 28 (top): © Gorodenkoff; p. 28 (bottom): © Maridav; p. 34: © Vasin Lee; p. 36: © Andrey Bayda; p. 40: © Ollyy; p. 46: © fizkes; p. 48: © fizkes; p. 49: © metamorworks; p. 50: © Rafal Olkis; p. 52: © sigur; p. 53: © Flamingo Images; p. 54: © Darren Brode; p. 55: © HUANSHENG XU; p. 57: © metamorworks; p. 59: © wavebreakmedia; p. 63: © Smile Fight; p. 65: © Scharfsinn; p. 71: © Mike Dexter; p. 73 (top): © Pavel Chagochkin; p. 73 (bottom): © Romolo Tavani; p. 74: © lev radin; p. 78: © 3Dsculptor; p. 79: © Petr Bonek; p. 80: © Jo Hunter; p. 83: © 360b; p. 85: © Aphelleon; p. 86: © Kathy Hutchins; p. 88: © photocritical; p. 93 (middle): © doomu; p. 94: © Rawpixel.com; p. 97: © wavebreakmedia; p. 98 (l): © Vereshchagin Dmitry; p. 98 (l, c): © AleksandarMilutinovic; p. 98 (c): © Bayurov Alexander; p. 98 (r, c): © Levent Konuk; p. 98 (r): © Ribah; p. 105: © FabrikaSimf; p. 106: © 7pic; p. 108: © mylisa; p. 111: © hopsalka; p. 112: © Stokkete; p. 117 (middle): © Irina Mir; p. 188: © l i g h t p o e t; p. 120: © klss; p. 124: © Brues; p. 128 (1): © FloridaStock; p. 128 (2, left): © gualtiero boffi; p. 128 (2, right): © sommai damrongpanich; p. 128 (4): © cynoclub; p. 128 (5): © Pakhnyushchy; p. 128 (6): © tea maeklong; p. 128 (7): © Eric Isselée; p. 131: © Krysja; p. 132: © Yurchanka Siarhei; p. 136: © Estrada Anton; p. 138: © AlexandreNunes; p. 139: © garetsworkshop; p. 141 (middle): © Marzolino; p. 142: © Rawpixel.com; p. 143: © LightField Studios; p. 144: © sezer66; p. 145: © Joyce Vincent; p. 147: © Marharyta Kovalenko; p. 151: © 4 PM production; p. 152: © GaudiLab; p. 155 (top): © fizkes; p. 161 (top): © nd3000; p. 163 (middle): © Olga Rosi; p. 166: © FS Stock; p. 167: © alaver; p. 168: © 24Novembers; p. 169: © VGstocksudio; p. 172: © John Roman Images; p. 173: © claudiozaccherini; p. 174: © Volt Collection; p. 177 (top): © Chinaview; p. 180 (top): © Jacob_09; p. 180 (bottom): © Timothy W. Stone; p. 185: © UfaBizPhoto.

THINKSTOCK

p. 8: © zimmytws; p. 13: © Wavebreakmedia Ltd; p. 18: © goldy; p. 32: © Jupiterimages; p. 35: © Anthony Brown; p. 38: © 2nix; p. 43 (top): © simonkr; p. 91 (top): © Fuse; p. 101: © 1971yes; p. 113: © koya79; p. 115 (top): © Monkey Business Images; p. 122: © dolgachov; p. 126 (top): © Chromatika Multimedia; p. 126 (middle): © piccaya; p. 128 (3, left): © Eric Isselée; p. 128 (3, right): © specnaz-s; p. 155 (bottom): © Jupiterimages; p. 156: © Antonio_Sanchez; p. 165: © Jupiterimages; p. 171: © ra2studio; p. 175: © montiannoowong; p. 177 (bottom): © Juergen Reinsch.

UNSPLASH

pp. vii, 44–45, 67 (top): © Eutah Mizushima.

AUDIO AND VIDEO CREDITS

CHAPTER 1

p. 6: "Ben Silbermann at Start-Up School" © Y Combinator. p. 19: "Start-Up and Slay" © Canadian Broadcasting Corporation. (2018, May 30).

CHAPTER 2

p. 32: "Students Create Their Own Dream Jobs" © Canadian Broadcasting Corporation. p. 37: "Crowdworkers" © Canadian Broadcasting Corporation. (2013, March 1).

CHAPTER 3

p. 49: "Autonomous Cars and the Future of Cities" © Canadian Broadcasting Corporation. (2013, September 20). p. 54: "Plugging In: The Future of Electric Cars" © Canadian Broadcasting Corporation.

CHAPTER 4

p. 73: "Science and Science Fiction with Andy Weir" © NASA. p. 86: "The First Moon Tourist" © Canadian Broadcasting Corporation.

CHAPTER 5

p. 97: "3D Printing" © Canadian Broadcasting Corporation. p. 104: "3D Printing: Making the Future" by J. A. Lewis. (Aug. 31, 2016). All content copyrighted 2017 by the President and Fellows of Harvard College, Harvard John A. Paulson School of Engineering and Applied Science.

CHAPTER 6

p. 120 "Activity Trackers and Apps" © Canadian Broadcasting Corporation. (2014, January 11). p. 131: "The Future of Human Enhancements" by G. Church, et al. (2018, May 21). "The Enhanced Human: Risks and Opportunities" is a co-presentation of the New York Academy of Sciences, the Aspen Brain Institute, and the Hastings Center. For further information: www.nyas.org.

CHAPTER 7

p. 144: "Gamification" © Canadian Broadcasting Corporation. (2014, September 4). p. 151: "New Models for Education" by D. Liechti. (2018, February 7). From *ChangeNOW Summit 2017: New Models for Education Innovators' Roundtable*." Changenow-summit.com.

CHAPTER 8

p. 167: "Technocreep" © Canadian Broadcasting Corporation. (2014, November 6). p. 180: "Human Rights" by Celebrate Humanity. Wissens Werte is a project by www.wissenswerte.e-politik.de realization edeos.org.

NOTES

08/2019